VOLUME 5

NEW TESTAMENT

THE NEW COLLEGEVILLE BIBLE COMMENTARY

THE ACTS OF THE APOSTLES

Dennis Hamm, S.J.

SERIES EDITOR

Daniel Durken, O.S.B.

LITURGICAL PRESS

Collegeville, Minnesota

www.litpress.org

Nihil obstat: Robert C. Harren, *Censor deputatus.*
Imprimatur: ✠ John F. Kinney, Bishop of St. Cloud, Minnesota, August 30, 2005.

Design by Ann Blattner.

Cover illustration: *Pentecost* by Donald Jackson. Natural hand-ground ink on calfskin vellum, 15-7/8" X 24-1/2." Copyright 2005 *The Saint John's Bible* and the Hill Museum & Manuscript Library at Saint John's University, United States of America. Scripture quotations are from the New Revised Standard Version of the Bible, Catholic Edition, copyright © 1989, 1993 National Council of the Churches of Christ in the United States of America. Used by permission. All rights reserved.

Photos: page 18, Corel Photos; page 50, Luke Steiner, O.S.B.; pages 73, 89, David Manahan, O.S.B.; page 80, Hellas Photos; page 122, Liturgical Press Photo.

Scriptures selections are taken from the New American Bible Copyright © 1991, 1986, 1970 by the Confraternity of Christian Doctrine, 3211 Fourth Street, NE, Washington, DC 20017-1194 and are used by license of copyright owner. All rights reserved. No part of the New American Bible may be reproduced in any form or by any means without permission in writing from the copyright owner.

	6	7	8	9

Library of Congress Cataloging-in-Publication Data

Hamm, M. Dennis.
    The Acts of the Apostles / Dennis Hamm.
        p. cm. — (The new Collegeville Bible commentary. New Testament ; v. 5)
    Summary: "Complete biblical texts with sound, scholarly based commentary that is written at a pastoral level; the Scripture translation is that of the New American Bible with Revised New Testament and Revised Psalms (1991)"—Provided by publisher.
    ISBN-13: 978-0-8146-2864-5 (pbk. : alk. paper)
    ISBN-10: 0-8146-2864-8 (pbk. : alk. paper)
    1. Bible. N.T. Acts—Commentaries. I. Title. II. Series.

BS2625.53.H36 2005
226.6'077—dc22   2005008466

CONTENTS

ABBREVIATIONS

Books of the Bible

Acts—Acts of the Apostles
Amos—Amos
Bar—Baruch
1 Chr—1 Chronicles
2 Chr—2 Chronicles
Col—Colossians
1 Cor—1 Corinthians
2 Cor—2 Corinthians
Dan—Daniel
Deut—Deuteronomy
Eccl (or Qoh)—Ecclesiastes
Eph—Ephesians
Esth—Esther
Exod—Exodus
Ezek—Ezekiel
Ezra—Ezra
Gal—Galatians
Gen—Genesis
Hab—Habakkuk
Hag—Haggai
Heb—Hebrews
Hos—Hosea
Isa—Isaiah
Jas—James
Jdt—Judith
Jer—Jeremiah
Job—Job
Joel—Joel
John—John
1 John—1 John
2 John—2 John
3 John—3 John
Jonah—Jonah
Josh—Joshua
Jude—Jude
Judg—Judges
1 Kgs—1 Kings

2 Kgs—2 Kings
Lam—Lamentations
Lev—Leviticus
Luke—Luke
1 Macc—1 Maccabees
2 Macc—2 Maccabees
Mal—Malachi
Mark—Mark
Matt—Matthew
Mic—Micah
Nah—Nahum
Neh—Nehemiah
Num—Numbers
Obad—Obadiah
1 Pet—1 Peter
2 Pet—2 Peter
Phil—Philippians
Phlm—Philemon
Prov—Proverbs
Ps(s)—Psalms
Rev—Revelation
Rom—Romans
Ruth—Ruth
1 Sam—1 Samuel
2 Sam—2 Samuel
Sir—Sirach
Song—Song of Songs
1 Thess—1 Thessalonians
2 Thess—2 Thessalonians
1 Tim—1 Timothy
2 Tim—2 Timothy
Titus—Titus
Tob—Tobit
Wis—Wisdom
Zech—Zechariah
Zeph—Zephaniah

The Acts of the Apostles

Welcome to a sequel. If the Acts of the Apostles were a contemporary film rather than an ancient document, they might call it "The Gospel of Luke: Part Two," for this book of the New Testament is clearly a sequel to the Third Gospel. The easiest way to recognize that fact is to read the first four verses of Luke's Gospel, where the author addresses one Theophilus (likely a new convert and possibly the sponsor of the publication—the one who paid the copyists) and then to flip forward to the opening phrase of Acts: "In the first book, Theophilus . . ." That should be enough to indicate that we are dealing with a two-volume work. Those who study and write about Luke's work are so conscious that his contribution to the New Testament canon—that is, the collection of books accepted by the church as inspired by God—is a two-volume project, deserving to be treated as a single masterpiece, that they commonly refer to it simply as Luke-Acts, as we shall do in this commentary.

This obvious fact of the unity of Luke-Acts has long escaped most readers because the conventional ordering of printed editions of the New Testament separates Luke's Gospel from its sequel by placing the Gospel of John between them. Those who chose that sequence had a perfectly good reason: the arrangement keeps the four canonical stories of Jesus together as a bundle. That way, Acts makes an appropriate bridge from the stories about Jesus to the letters of Paul. But this arrangement also has a downside: it has accidentally distracted readers from recognizing the continuity between the two parts of Luke's work.

During the last third of the twentieth century, biblical scholars have focused less on the study of discrete segments of texts and more on the form and meaning of entire documents. That focus has produced a fresh appreciation of the integrity and artistry of the work now commonly called Luke-Acts.

How does Luke himself understand his project? Luke expresses his intentions regarding the whole of Luke-Acts in the four-verse introduction at the head of his Gospel.

> [1]Since many have undertaken to compile a narrative of the events that have been fulfilled among us, [2]just as those who were eyewitnesses from the beginning and ministers of the word have handed them down to us, [3]I too have decided, after investigating everything accurately anew, to write it down in an orderly sequence for you, most excellent Theophilus, [4]so that you may realize the certainty of the teachings you have received.

Notice that the subject of his work is "the events that have been fulfilled among us." The phrase "events fulfilled" suggests that those events were not simply happenings but truly fulfillments of the Scriptures of Israel. The "us" in question is the Christian community of Luke's own time, a group far enough removed in time (at least by forty or fifty years) from the life, death, and resurrection of Jesus that they needed the testimony of eyewitnesses and preachers of the word to learn about those events. And yet the "us" was in such continuity with that first generation of Christians (the eyewitnesses) that those events could be understood as fulfilled among *us*. In other words, Luke's audience could still think of the past events as having been fulfilled among *them*. This also applies to subsequent readers, including us.

Did Luke think that such "fulfillment" events were still occurring in his own time? Yes. Other parts of Luke-Acts indicate this awareness quite clearly. Consider Jesus' final words at the close of Luke's Gospel: "Thus it is written that the Messiah would suffer and rise from the dead on the third day, *and that repentance, for the forgiveness of sins, would be preached in his name to all the nations, beginning from Jerusalem*" (Luke 24:46-47, emphasis added). Notice that what is said to fulfill the Scriptures here is not only the death and resurrection of the Messiah but also the preaching of repentance in the name of Jesus to all the nations, which is precisely what Acts is all about. So "the events that have been fulfilled among us" include not only the story of Jesus (told in the Third Gospel) but also the story of the church (the subject of Acts) as it continues to unfold in Luke's own generation. By the extension implied in his vision, our generation is included as well. This awareness of the end-time fulfillment occurring in the time of the church comes through strongly in an assertion in Peter's speech in Acts 3:24: "Moreover, all the prophets who spoke, from Samuel and those afterwards, also announced these days."

Are there other clues to the unity of Luke-Acts? There are many. Take, for example, the words that Gabriel speaks to Mary at the annunciation.

> "He will be great and will be called Son of the Most High, and the Lord God will give him the throne of David his father, and he will rule over the house of Jacob forever . . ." (Luke 1:32-33).

It is instructive to see what happens to those predictions throughout the remainder of Luke-Acts. In the world of first-century Judaism, the word about Jesus' inheriting David's throne meant becoming the Messiah, the end-time political and religious leader of a restored people of Israel. When does Luke show Jesus taking up that role? Certainly not in the Gospel. Nowhere in Luke's narrative of Jesus's life, death, and resurrection does Jesus become king in that conventional sense. Indeed, talk of kingship occurs only ironically—in the accusations of the Sanhedrin, in the mockery of the leaders and soldiers under the cross, and in the inscription on the cross: "This is the king of the Jews." But the implication of these ironic references is that Jesus has failed to inherit the throne of David in the conventional sense. His kingship turns out to be far grander than that.

The reader has to begin reading the second volume, the Acts of the Apostles, to learn Luke's understanding of how Jesus inherits David's throne. In Peter's speech at Pentecost, we hear Peter recite a psalm of David, Psalm 16, in which the speaker of the prayer expresses the hope that his flesh will not "see corruption." Peter then asserts that these words of David were not spoken about himself but about the Messiah. Psalm 16, Peter says, must be interpreted in the light of 2 Samuel 7:12 and Psalm 132:11 in a way that points only to Jesus. Jesus now reigns over end-time Israel, not from an earthly throne in Jerusalem but as risen Lord of the Christian community. That is just one example of the careful continuity between the Gospel of Luke and the Acts of the Apostles. This commentary will highlight many more such links between the first and second parts of Luke's two-volume work.

Why did Luke's readers need a sequel? These preliminary observations may begin to suggest some of the reasons why Luke added a sequel to his new edition of the story of Jesus.

A church increasingly composed of non-Jews (Gentiles) needed help in understanding how Gentiles could claim the heritage of Israel. Luke tells the story of the church to demonstrate that their experience is the fruition of "the light to the nations" (Isa 49:6) that the People of God was always meant to be.

People living after the generation of the original eyewitnesses needed a way of understanding how the life of Jesus still had relevance in their own lives. Luke shows how the life of Christians, individually and communally, is always some kind of replay of the life of Jesus. Thus Stephen's death parallels Jesus' death, and the travels and trials of Paul mirror the travels and trials of Jesus.

As a community spreading throughout the Roman Empire, the church needed an account of itself that demonstrated honorable roots (origins in the ancient people of Israel) and posed no political threat to Roman law and order. And so Luke stresses biblical fulfillment and underscores the innocence of Jesus and his followers in the courts of Roman officials.

A growing church needed models for interacting with the worlds it was encountering. And so Luke told its early history not simply as reminiscences of "the way we were" but in the form of episodes that could model "the way we *are.*" Indeed, that is why the Acts of the Apostles has been of permanent value to the church. While we can never succeed in simply replicating the early days of the church, we can always find reminders of what has been permanently important to the life of the church in Luke's portrayal of those early days.

What are we to make of all those short speeches? A good third of the content of the Acts of the Apostles consists of brief speeches. Often readers have taken these to be something like "tapes" of the apostolic preaching. Intense study of the Greek-writing historians of the first century has, however, led scholars to another conclusion. One of the tools of history writing in the Mediterranean world of those days was the composition of speeches put on the lips of key figures to interpret the meaning of the events narrated. In other words, even when Hellenistic (Greek) historians had verbatim records of what an important person said on a particular occasion, they would consider it part of good history writing to use the benefit of hindsight, along with the sources at their disposal, and compose a speech that captured the essential truth of what was happening. Most Lukan scholars judge that the speeches in Acts represent that kind of history writing, that is, Luke, drawing upon the tradition handed down from the apostles, composes speeches and puts them on the lips of Peter, Paul, and Stephen to explain to his readers the meaning of the history he is telling.

To those of us who thought we were hearing in those speeches the very words of Peter and Paul, this way of understanding the speeches was, at first, disappointing. But in the end, taking Luke to be writing speeches in the manner of his peer historians makes better sense of the material. For each of those speeches makes more sense as addressed to Luke's readers rather than as addressed to the audience within the plot line of the narrative. Indeed, the speeches build on one another and presume an audience that has read the Third Gospel and the rest of the Acts of the Apostles.

What we have in those cameo speeches, then, is not a set of tapes that we have to sort out for ourselves (like editors working with Richard

8

Nixon's White House tapes); rather, what we have are Luke's authoritative interpretations of the early history of the church. Because of their content, they also give us examples of the early church's use of Scripture in proclaiming the good news. At the end of the day, this is a more satisfying and instructive way of reading those speeches. This commentary aims to make that apparent.

Outline. Many commentators have observed that Jesus' words to the disciples before his ascension contain a kind of outline of Acts: "You will be my witnesses in Jerusalem, throughout Judea and Samaria, and to the ends of the earth" (Acts 1:8). That observation is illustrated in the following outline:

I.   The Risen Christ and the Restoration of Israel in Jerusalem (1:1–8:3).
II. The Mission in Judea and Samaria (8:4–9:43).
III. The Inauguration of the Gentile Mission (10:1–15:35).
IV. The Mission of Paul to the Ends of the Earth (15:36–28:31).

This way of outlining the major movements of Luke's history also reflects one of the main texts from the Scriptures that he uses to interpret what is going on in the early history of the church:

> For now the LORD has spoken
>   who formed me as his servant from the womb,
> That Jacob may be brought back to him
>   and Israel gathered to him;
> And I am made glorious in the sight of the LORD,
>   and my God is now my strength!
> It is too little, he says, for you to be my servant,
>   to raise up the tribes of Jacob,
>   and restore the survivors of Israel;
> I will make you a light to the nations,
>   that my salvation may reach to the ends of the
>   earth. (Isa 49:5-6)

Notice that this prophecy about Servant/Israel entails two stages: first, the restoration of Israel (the twelve tribes of Jacob); second, becoming a "light to the nations." In the Acts of the Apostles, Luke shows how this prophecy is fulfilled.

Isaiah's first stage, the end-time restoration of Israel, unfolds in the first two movements in Acts—first in the formation of the Jerusalem community out of Jews from all nations (1:1–8:3), then in their outreach to Jews in the surrounding area and to Samaritans (8:4–9:43).

Isaiah's second stage, becoming a "light to the nations," unfolds in two further movements—first in the inauguration of the mission to the Gentiles (10:1–15:35), then in Paul's mission to "the ends of the earth" (15:36–28:31).

This commentary will highlight the two continuities sketched in this introduction: (1) the continuity between the story of Jesus and the story of the church, and (2) the continuity between the Christian story as a whole and the longer story of Israel's life with God, as told in the Greek version of the Hebrew Scriptures. The importance of this approach was underscored by the recent document of the Pontifical Biblical Commission, "The Jewish People and Their Sacred Scriptures in the Christian Bible" (Vatican City: Libreria Editrice Vaticana, 2002; available at http://www.libreriaeditricevaticana.com).

Although the format of this commentary does not allow for footnotes, the author's dependence on prior commentators will be obvious to those familiar with Lukan scholarship. Readers who wish to pursue their study of Luke-Acts more deeply should consult the following: Luke Timothy Johnson, *The Acts of the Apostles* (Collegeville, Minn.: Liturgical Press, 1992); James D. G. Dunn, *The Acts of the Apostles* (Valley Forge, Pa.: Trinity Press, 1996); Joseph A. Fitzmyer, S.J., *The Acts of the Apostles,* Anchor Bible 31 (New York: Doubleday, 1998); and Ben Witherington, III, *The Acts of the Apostles* (Grand Rapids, Mich.: William B. Eerdmans, 1998).

Now let us begin to read Luke's sequel.

The Acts of the Apostles

I. The Preparation for the Christian Mission

1 **The Promise of the Spirit.** ¹In the first book, Theophilus, I dealt with all that Jesus did and taught ²until the day he was taken up, after giving instructions through the holy Spirit to the apostles whom he had chosen. ³He presented himself alive to them by many proofs after he had suffered, appearing to them during forty days and speaking about the kingdom of God. ⁴While meeting with them, he enjoined them not to depart from Jerusalem, but to wait for "the promise of the Father about which you have heard me speak; ⁵for John

---

THE RISEN CHRIST
AND THE RESTORATION OF ISRAEL IN JERUSALEM

Acts 1:1–8:3

Luke shows how Jesus' mission to initiate the end-time restoration of Israel finds expression in the emergent, Spirit-filled Christian community in Jerusalem.

1:1-5 Introduction: "As I was saying, Theophilus . . ."

Luke introduces this sequel to his Gospel by addressing Theophilus, as he did in the prologue to his Gospel (Luke 1:1-4), indicating that this is a continuation of the same project described there. Literally, the Greek of verse 1 says, "I dealt with all that Jesus *began* to do and teach," implying that Acts will treat what Jesus *continues* to do and teach through the apostolic church. And the phrase "through the holy Spirit" more naturally modifies "chosen"—that is, "after giving instructions to the apostles whom he had chosen through the holy Spirit." For Luke, alone among the Synoptic writers, notes that Jesus chose the Twelve after spending the night in prayer (Luke 6:12-13), which for Luke often precedes a special

---

▶ This symbol indicates a cross reference number in the *Catechism of the Catholic Church*. See page 130 for number citations.

baptized with water, but in a few days you will be baptized with the holy Spirit."

The Ascension of Jesus. ⁶When they had gathered together they asked him, "Lord, are you at this time going to restore the kingdom to Israel?" ⁷He answered them, "It is not for you to know the times or seasons that the Father has established by his own authority. ⁸But you will receive power when the holy Spirit comes upon you, and you will be my witnesses in Jerusalem, throughout Judea and Samaria, and to the ends of the earth." ⁹When he had said this, as they were looking on, he was lifted up, and a cloud took him from their sight. ¹⁰While they were looking intently at the sky as he was going, suddenly two men dressed in white garments stood beside them. ¹¹They said, "Men of Galilee, why are you standing there looking at the sky? This Jesus who has been taken up from

---

empowerment by the Spirit (see Luke 3:21, leading to 4:18; Acts 1:14, leading to 2:1-4; and Acts 4:23-31).

As in the Gospel, the centerpiece of Jesus' teaching remains the kingdom of God. Jesus' reference to "the promise of the Father" alludes to at least three passages in the Third Gospel: (1) Luke 11:13: "If you then, who are wicked, know how to give good gifts to your children, how much more will the Father in heaven give the holy Spirit to those who ask him?"; (2) Luke 12:32: "Do not be afraid any longer, little flock, for your Father is pleased to give you the kingdom"; (3) Luke 24:49: "And [behold] I am sending the promise of my Father upon you; but stay in the city until you are clothed with power from on high." The gift of the Spirit at Pentecost will also signal a further manifestation of the kingdom of God already inaugurated in the ministry of Jesus (see Luke 11:20 and 17:21).

Linking this blessing with John the Baptist's prophecy about being "baptiz[ed in] the holy Spirit" (Luke 3:16) also ties this promise to Ezekiel's promise of a cleansing restoration of the people of Israel that will accompany the gift of the divine Spirit (Ezek 36:24-27).

1:6-12 The ascension of Jesus

Since the disciples are Jews who have identified Jesus as their long-awaited Messiah, it is reasonable for them to ask if Jesus will now restore the kingdom to Israel (v. 6). After all, he has been speaking to them for forty days about the kingdom of God, which, in the common expectation of the day, is supposed to be a restoration of the nation to what it was when David reigned a millennium before. Jesus does not deny the appropriateness of the question; he simply refuses to reveal to them the divinely decreed schedule (v. 7). Jesus also reinterprets their implied notion of the kingdom; it is not going to be a matter of nationalism but a new kind of

you into heaven will return in the same way as you have seen him going into heaven." ¹²Then they returned to Jerusalem from the mount called Olivet, which is near Jerusalem, a sabbath day's journey away.

The First Community in Jerusalem. ¹³When they entered the city they went to the upper room where they were staying, Peter and John and James and Andrew, Philip and Thomas, Bartholomew and Matthew, James son

---

unity empowered by the holy Spirit, as foreshadowed by the new "family" portrayed in Luke 8:1-21.

In this, Jesus echoes what he had said to them on Easter Sunday (Luke 24:49). When he tells them that the Spirit's power will enable them to be his witnesses from Jerusalem "to the ends of the earth" (v. 8), he alludes to Isaiah 49:6, where the Lord tells his Servant that he will not only restore the tribes of Jacob but will also be a light to the nations, "that my salvation will reach to the ends of the earth."

Although the traditional word for the withdrawal of Jesus' physical presence from the apostles is "the ascension," it might be more accurate to describe Luke's description of this event as an "assumption," since the author portrays it as an act of the Father. To describe this departure, Luke draws upon the biblical traditions about the assumptions of Enoch (Gen 5:23-24; Sir 49:14b) and Elijah (2 Kgs 2:9-11; Sir 48:9). To interpret the event, he adds what have been called "apocalyptic stage props"—the movement upward into the heavens, a cloud as vehicle, and the interpreting angels.

This is Luke's second account of the ascension. The first account, given at the end of Luke's Gospel (24:50-51), sets the event on Easter Sunday and describes Jesus in details that recall the description of the high priest Simon II in Sirach 50:1-24. Like Simon, Jesus' presence occasions worship (Sir 50:17, 22); he raises his hands and pronounces a blessing (Sir 50:20), and this is followed by references to the community's blessing God and rejoicing in the temple (Sir 50:22-23). In so doing, Jesus is acting like the temple priest at the end of the daily Whole-Offering (also called the Tamid, or "regular," service; Exod 29:38-42; Num 2:1-10). And within the Gospel narrative, Jesus is doing what the priest Zechariah was unable to do at the end of the Tamid service, whose incense ritual is the scenario briefly portrayed at the beginning of Luke's Gospel. By alluding in this manner to Sirach 50, Luke was celebrating Jesus the way Ben Sira celebrated Simon II as the climax of his Praise of the Ancestors (Sirach 44–50). For Luke, it is Jesus, not Simon II, who is the climax of Israel's history; and so Luke chooses to end his first volume by portraying Jesus' departure on Easter Sunday with those overtones.

◄ of Alphaeus, Simon the Zealot, and Judas son of James. [14]All these devoted themselves with one accord to prayer, together with some women, and Mary the mother of Jesus, and his brothers.

The Choice of Judas's Successor. [15]During those days Peter stood up in the midst of the brothers (there was a group of about one hundred and twenty persons in the one place). He said, [16]"My brothers, the scripture had to be fulfilled which the holy Spirit spoke beforehand through the mouth of David, concerning Judas, who was the guide for those who arrested Jesus. [17]He was numbered among us and was allotted a share in this ministry. [18]He bought a parcel of land with the wages of his iniquity, and falling headlong, he burst open in the middle, and all his insides spilled out. [19]This became known to everyone who lived in Jerusalem, so

Why, then, does Luke take the liberty to narrate this event so differently as he begins his second volume? Some scholars suggest that in Acts Luke has expanded the time frame of Luke 24 to the round (and biblically symbolic) number forty, in order to associate the ascension closely with the outpouring of the Spirit on the fiftieth day, Pentecost (the Jewish feast of the giving of the Law on Mount Sinai). The apocalyptic stage props serve four purposes: (1) to recall the transfiguration (Luke 9:18-36, another mountain episode, when the disciples could not pray, as now they can); (2) to look forward to the outpouring of the Spirit and the mission that follows; (3) to recount the departure of Jesus in a way that recalls 2 Kings 2:9-12 (another narrative about the transmission of spirit for prophetic succession); and (4) to point toward the final coming (described already in Luke 21:27 as coming "in a cloud," alluding to the cloud imagery of Daniel 7:13, but in the singular, to prepare for Acts 1:9). Thus Luke is able to speak of one reality, the final departure of Jesus from his assembled followers, from two interpretive points of view. Luke 24 alludes to the ascension as a fitting ending of the story of Jesus; Acts 1 narrates the same event as the beginning of the story of the mission of the Church, initiated by the risen Lord and empowered by the gift of the Spirit.

1:13-26 The community gathers to restore "the Twelve" by electing Matthias

The apostles (minus Judas Iscariot) whom Luke had carefully called "the eleven" at Luke 24:33 gather with the "women, and Mary the mother of Jesus, and his brothers" (v. 14). This group, numbered at 120 in verse 15 (notice the multiple of 12), comprises the nucleus of the church that will become the heart of restored Israel in chapter 2.

"The women" no doubt included Mary Magdalene, Joanna, Susanna, and Mary the mother of James, and the many other women who had ac-

that the parcel of land was called in their language 'Akeldama,' that is, Field of Blood. [20]For it is written in the Book of Psalms:

> 'Let his encampment become
> desolate,
> and may no one dwell in it.'

And:

> 'May another take his office.'

[21]Therefore, it is necessary that one of the men who accompanied us the whole time the Lord Jesus came and went among us, [22]beginning from the baptism of John until the day on which he was taken up from us, become with us a witness to his resurrection." [23]So they proposed two, Joseph called Barsabbas, who was also known as Justus, and Matthias. [24]Then they prayed, "You, Lord, who know the hearts of all, show which one of these two you have chosen [25]to take the place in this apostolic ministry from which Judas turned away to go to his own place." [26]Then

---

companied Jesus and the Twelve and had "provided for them out of their resources" (Luke 8:3). They are the ones "who had come from Galilee with him" (Luke 23:55) and, coming to anoint the body of Jesus in the tomb, discovered it empty and became the first witnesses to the resurrection (Luke 24:10, 22-23).

His "brothers" are the very ones who, together with Jesus' mother, were last seen in Luke 8:19-21, standing at the edge of a crowd around Jesus when he said, "My mother and my brothers are those who hear the word of God and act on it" (v. 21). Whatever the ambiguity of their status then, now they are at the center of the believing community. Like Jesus after the water immersion by John and before his special anointing by the Spirit (Luke 3:21), the community is immersed in prayer.

Jesus' prayer that Simon Peter, even after denying Jesus, will turn back and strengthen his brothers (Luke 22:32) begins to be fulfilled, as Peter now asserts his leadership (Acts 1:15).

The first agenda item to be addressed by the community is the replacement of Judas Iscariot, who had been "numbered" among the core group (v. 17). Because of the symbolic meaning of Jesus' choice of twelve, indicating the restoration of the twelve tribes of the people of God, "the eleven" (Luke 24:33) must again become the Twelve.

The importance of the number twelve becomes clear when one recalls the words of Jesus at the Last Supper: "And I confer a kingdom on you, just as my Father has conferred one on me, that you may eat and drink at my table in my kingdom; and you will sit on thrones judging the twelve tribes of Israel" (Luke 22:29-30). Whatever Matthew's parallel saying may mean in the context of his Gospel (Matt 19:28), for Luke this is a reference to the leadership of the Twelve in the Jerusalem church after Pentecost.

they gave lots to them, and the lot fell upon Matthias, and he was counted with the eleven apostles.

◄ **2 The Coming of the Spirit.** ¹When the time for Pentecost was fulfilled, they were all in one place together. ²And suddenly there came from the sky a noise like a strong driving wind, and it filled the entire house in which they

◄ were. ³Then there appeared to them tongues as of fire, which parted and came to rest on each one of them. ⁴And they were all filled with the holy Spirit and began to speak in different tongues, as the Spirit enabled them to proclaim.

⁵Now there were devout Jews from every nation under heaven staying in Jerusalem. ⁶At this sound, they gathered in a large crowd, but they were confused because each one heard them speaking in his own language. ⁷They were astounded, and in amazement they asked, "Are not all these people who are speaking Galileans? ⁸Then how does each of us hear them in his own native language? ⁹We are Parthians, Medes, and Elamites, inhabitants of Mesopotamia, Judea and Cappadocia, Pontus and Asia, ¹⁰Phrygia and Pamphylia, Egypt and the districts of Libya

---

"Judging" here has the sense it has in the book of Judges, which features twelve charismatic leaders who led the tribes of Israel before the time of the monarchy. The reconstituted Twelve will similarly "judge" (that is, exert Spirit-filled leadership among) the reconstituted people of Israel after Pentecost.

The way the words of Peter (1:16-20) and the prayer of the community (1:24-25) speak of Judas's death is full of irony. Abandoning a community that will soon express its unity and detachment from material possessions by selling fields, with no one calling anything his own, Judas invested his blood money in a field ("turned away . . . to his own place," v. 25) and died there in a horrible, isolated death. Whereas Matthew's account of Judas's death (Matt 27:5) parallels the suicide-by-hanging of David's betrayer Ahithophel (2 Sam 17:23), Luke's version reflects the punitive death-by-falling that was Antiochus IV's end (2 Macc 9:12-14).

The community makes sure that Judas's replacement will be a qualified witness to the resurrection by choosing two candidates who were present with Jesus from the baptism of John through the ascension. Then, having done their human best, they put the final choice out of their hands, leaving it up to God through the device of casting lots. Thus Matthias is chosen to restore the Twelve.

2:1-13 The coming of the Spirit

Pentēcostēs (literally "fiftieth") is the Greek name for the Israelite feast of Weeks (*Shavuʾot* in Hebrew). The second of the three classical pilgrim feasts of Israel—Unleavened Bread/Passover, Weeks, and Booths (see

The Upper Room, traditional site of the Last Supper

near Cyrene, as well as travelers from Rome, [11]both Jews and converts to Judaism, Cretans and Arabs, yet we hear them speaking in our own tongues of the mighty acts of God." [12]They were all astounded and bewildered, and said to one another, "What does this mean?"

[13]But others said, scoffing, "They have had too much new wine."

II. The Mission in Jerusalem

Peter's Speech at Pentecost. [14]Then Peter stood up with the Eleven, raised his voice, and proclaimed to them,

---

Exod 23:14-17; 34:22; Deut 16:16)—the feast of Weeks was called "Fiftieth" in Greek because it occurred seven weeks, or fifty days, after the feast of Unleavened Bread/Passover. Originally an agricultural feast celebrating the end of the grain harvest, Pentecost eventually came to be associated with the giving of the Law at Sinai.

Luke narrates the Pentecost events in words and images that evoke the revelation at Mount Sinai. The reconstituted Twelve (among the 120) are gathered like the twelve tribes at Sinai. The sounds from heaven, the filling of the *whole* house (like the shaking of the *whole* mountain in Exodus 19:18), and the fire recall the theophany (appearance of God) at Sinai. The tongues of fire symbolize the reality that the powerful presence of God (like fire) will find expression in human words, the prophetic ministry of the disciples. The appearance of fire also corresponds to John the Baptist's prediction that Jesus would baptize "with the holy Spirit and fire" (Luke 3:16). In the fuller sweep of the narrative, the parallel between Jesus and Moses is evident in that Jesus ascends with a cloud (1:9) and then mediates the gift of the prophetic word of God to the people (2:4, 11, 18, 33). Thus Luke underscores the fact that on the feast of the giving of the Law (the privileged communication of God's word) comes the end-time gift of the holy Spirit to empower a fresh expression of the divine word in the ministry of the apostles.

The list of nations from which the Jewish pilgrims and converts come symbolizes the future implications of what is happening here. By highlighting this inclusive gathering, Luke proclaims that this is in fact the fulfillment of the expected end-time ingathering of Israel. The Pentecostal gift is destined for Jews first, but then also for the "ends of the earth" (Acts 1:8), "those far off" (2:39; see Isa 57:19).

When Luke says that they "were *confused* because each one heard them speaking in his own language" (v. 6, emphasis added), he appears to be alluding to the story of the tower of Babel (in its Septuagint version, that is, the Greek translation of the Hebrew Old Testament). Whereas Genesis 11 tells of a sinful people who wish to make a name for themselves and are

"You who are Jews, indeed all of you staying in Jerusalem. Let this be known to you, and listen to my words. [15]These people are not drunk, as you suppose, for it is only nine o'clock in the morning. [16]No, this is what was spoken through the prophet Joel:

[17]'It will come to pass in the last days,' God says,
'that I will pour out a portion of my spirit upon all flesh.

Your sons and your daughters shall prophesy,
your young men shall see visions,
your old men shall dream dreams.
[18]Indeed, upon my servants and my handmaids
I will pour out a portion of my spirit in those days,
and they shall prophesy.
[19]And I will work wonders in the heavens above

---

scattered in confusion and lose their ability to communicate (literally "to *hear* one another"), Acts 2 tells of a people of many languages who gather, are "confused" by a new ability to "hear," and are empowered to become a new community as they repent of their sins and call upon the name of the Lord. The likelihood of the allusion becomes even stronger when one notes that the name Babel is rendered *Sygchysis* ("Confusion") in the Septuagint.

2:14-36 Peter explains: the Spirit of God is restoring end-time Israel, and the crucified Jesus is its risen Messiah and Lord!

In this speech of Peter to the festival crowd, Luke employs a kind of biblical interpretation that the Dead Sea Scrolls have taught us to call a *pesher*. The word *pesher* is simply Aramaic for "interpretation." But in the hands of the Essenes, an ascetical community that lived at Qumran, a *pesher* meant understanding a biblical passage as fulfilled in the present or recent history of their own community. Luke now has Peter explain the significance of the Pentecost events in a series of such *peshers*.

After a deft and humorous remark about the enthusiastic behavior of the community (they are not drunk; it's only nine in the morning, v. 15), Peter quotes Joel 3:1-5, joining it with a crucial phrase from the Greek version of Isaiah 2:2 ("in the last days"). He says, in effect, that what has been happening in Jerusalem is the fulfillment of these end-time prophecies. Whereas Israel had experienced a special infusion of God's spirit on an occasional king or prophet, now "in the last days" the gift of the prophetic spirit has been made available in a surprisingly inclusive way, transcending gender ("your sons and daughters," "my servants and my handmaids") and age ("young," "old," v. 17).

In true *pesher* fashion, Peter proceeds to apply specific phrases to recent and current events. He interprets the phrase "wonders . . . and signs" of verse 19 as the wondrous deeds God had done through Jesus. As

19

and signs on the earth below:
blood, fire, and a cloud of
smoke.
²⁰The sun shall be turned to
darkness,
and the moon to blood,
before the coming of the
great and splendid
day of the Lord,
²¹and it shall be that everyone shall
be saved who calls on
the name of the Lord.'
²²You who are Israelites, hear these
words. Jesus the Nazorean was a man
commended to you by God with
mighty deeds, wonders, and signs,
which God worked through him in
your midst, as you yourselves know.
²³This man, delivered up by the set plan
and foreknowledge of God, you killed,

using lawless men to crucify him. ²⁴But
God raised him up, releasing him from
the throes of death, because it was impossible for him to be held by it. ²⁵For
David says of him:

'I saw the Lord ever before me,
with him at my right hand I
shall not be disturbed.
²⁶Therefore my heart has been glad
and my tongue has exulted;
my flesh, too, will dwell in
hope,
²⁷because you will not abandon my
soul to the netherworld,
nor will you suffer your holy
one to see corruption.
²⁸You have made known to me the
paths of life;
you will fill me with joy in your
presence.'

---

his story continues to unfold, it will become clear that Joel's reference to those "who calls on the name of the Lord" will be applied to those who call upon the name of the Lord *Jesus* in Christian faith (see 9:14, 21; 22:16). And so the quotation from Joel 3, fortified by Isaiah 2:2, interprets *what time it is:* it is the inauguration of the long-awaited end-time, begun by God in Jesus and continued by God through the church.

But this outpouring of the Spirit on the community of believers is more than a sign of the end times; it is also a sign of the resurrection and enthronement of Jesus. To make this point, Luke (through Peter) enlists the last third of Psalm 16, which contains the clause " . . . you will not abandon my soul to the nether world, / nor will you suffer your holy one to undergo corruption" (1970 version). With the traditional understand-ing that all the psalms come from David, Peter argues that since David himself died and therefore *his* flesh obviously "saw corruption," the words must apply to someone else. Add to this the prophecy of Psalm 132:11 that God would set one of David's descendants on his throne, and these texts turn out to apply to the Messiah *in his resurrection*. It is in this sense, as risen king of restored Israel, that Jesus can be called "the Anointed One" ("Messiah" in Hebrew, "Christ" in Greek).

Then, to show how the risen Jesus is entitled also to the name "Lord" (used in the quotation from Joel 3 in Acts 2:21), Peter enlists the first verse

²⁹My brothers, one can confidently say to you about the patriarch David that he died and was buried, and his tomb is in our midst to this day. ³⁰But since he was a prophet and knew that God had sworn an oath to him that he would set one of his descendants upon his throne, ³¹he foresaw and spoke of the resurrection of the Messiah, that neither was he abandoned to the netherworld nor did his flesh see corruption. ³²God raised this Jesus; of this we are all witnesses. ◄ ³³Exalted at the right hand of God, he received the promise of the holy Spirit from the Father and poured it forth, as ◄ you [both] see and hear. ³⁴For David did not go up into heaven, but he himself said:

'The Lord said to my Lord,
"Sit at my right hand
³⁵until I make your enemies
    your footstool." '

³⁶Therefore let the whole house of Israel ► know for certain that God has made him both Lord and Messiah, this Jesus whom you crucified."

³⁷Now when they heard this, they were cut to the heart, and they asked Peter and the other apostles, "What are we to do, my brothers?" ³⁸Peter [said] ► to them, "Repent and be baptized, every one of you, in the name of Jesus Christ for the forgiveness of your sins; and you will receive the gift of the holy Spirit. ³⁹For the promise is made to you and to your children and to all those far

---

of Psalm 110: "The LORD said to my Lord, 'Sit at my right hand / till I make your enemies your footstool'" (1970 version). The final verse of the speech (2:36) summarizes the whole speech succinctly.

2:37-41 The response to the proclamation

When the people ask Peter what they should do, he invites them to repent and be baptized in the name of the Lord Jesus (which, in the light of the preceding speech, means belief in the resurrection of Jesus). And when Peter promises that they will receive the "gift of the holy Spirit," we now understand that the events of Acts 2 are the fulfillment of John the Baptist's promise that one mightier than he would baptize "in the holy Spirit and fire" (Luke 3:16; see also Acts 1:5). Mission to the Gentiles is already glimpsed when Peter joins "you and . . . your children" with "and to all *those far off*" (Isaiah's phrase for Gentiles in Isaiah 57:19, emphasis added). Jewish and Gentile Christians alike will qualify as those ". . . whom the LORD shall call" (Joel 3:5).

2:42-47 The first Christian community

Although the portrait of the *koinōnia*, or communal life, of the Jerusalem Christian community (vv. 42-47) has often been used to illustrate the ideals of vowed religious life, Luke clearly means it to portray the Christian community of Jerusalem as restored Israel. Each of the details is powerfully suggestive, describing who they are and what they are about.

off, whomever the Lord our God will call." [40]He testified with many other arguments, and was exhorting them, "Save yourselves from this corrupt generation." [41]Those who accepted his message were baptized, and about three thousand persons were added that day.

Communal Life. [42]They devoted themselves to the teaching of the apostles and to the communal life, to the breaking of the bread and to the prayers. [43]Awe came upon everyone, and many wonders and signs were done through the apostles. [44]All who believed were together and had all things in common; [45]they would sell their property and possessions and divide them among all according to each one's need. [46]Every day they devoted themselves to meeting together in the temple area and to breaking bread in their homes. They ate their meals with exultation and sincerity of heart, [47]praising God and enjoying favor with all the people. And every day the Lord

---

The "teaching of the apostles" to which they devote themselves no doubt refers to the teaching of Jesus and the kind of biblical interpretation regarding Jesus just displayed in Peter's Pentecost speech. Since "the breaking of the bread" (v. 42) refers to the practice of the Lord's Supper, "the prayers" are likely the traditional prayers of Jewish life, such as the *Shema* (Deut 6:4-9; note the reference to the Christians regularly gathering in the temple area in verse 46, presumably for prayer, as in 3:1). That the apostles are said to perform "wonders and signs" (v. 43) reinforces the continuity between their ministry and that of Jesus, just described as commended by God with "wonders and signs" in verse 22. Their sense of mutual service (see Luke 22:25-27) leads them spontaneously to share their possessions, even to sell property to meet one another's needs (v. 45). That they continue to meet in the temple area is consistent with the description, at the end of Luke's Gospel, that "they were continually [or regularly] in the temple praising God" (Luke 24:53). The Jewish Christians' allegiance to Jesus as Lord and Messiah has not meant severance from the life of the temple.

Finally, notice that verse 47b describes this Christian communal life as "being saved"—an explication of a phrase from Joel quoted in verse 21 ("everyone *shall be saved* who calls on the name of the Lord"; emphasis added). The awe (*phobos*, literally "fear") that comes upon everyone is reminiscent of the fear that God sent upon the nations as they witnessed the progress of the Exodus and Conquest (Exod 15:16; 23:27; Deut 2:25; 11:25; 32:25; Josh 2:9). This awe is a continuation of the people's response to the new Exodus already begun in the story of Jesus (see Luke 1:12, 65; 2:9; 5:26; 7:16; 8:37; 21:26).

added to their number those who were being saved.

3 Cure of a Crippled Beggar. ¹Now Peter and John were going up to the temple area for the three o'clock hour of prayer. ²And a man crippled from birth was carried and placed at the gate of the temple called "the Beautiful Gate" every day to beg for alms from the people who entered the temple. ³When he saw Peter and John about to go into the temple, he asked for alms. ⁴But Peter looked intently at him, as did John, and said, "Look at us." ⁵He paid attention to them, expecting to receive something from them. ⁶Peter said, "I have neither silver nor gold, but what I do have I give you: in the name of Jesus Christ the Nazorean, [rise and] walk." ⁷Then Peter took him by the right hand and raised him up, and immediately his feet and ankles grew strong. ⁸He leaped up, stood, and walked around, and went into the temple with them, walking and jumping and praising God. ⁹When all the people saw him walking and praising God, ¹⁰they recognized him as the one who used to sit begging at the Beautiful Gate of the temple, and they were filled with amazement and astonishment at what had happened to him.

Peter's Speech. ¹¹As he clung to Peter and John, all the people hurried in

---

This cameo picture of the life of the Jerusalem Christian community reflects the fulfillment of the jubilee theme struck in the quotation of Isaiah 61:2 at Luke 4:19.

3:1-26 The healing of the man born lame and Peter's explanation

Having referred to "many wonders and signs worked through the apostles" (2:43), Luke now describes in detail one such sign—the healing of the lame man at the temple gate. As in the case of the Pentecost events, he also provides a speech that interprets the significance of that sign.

Consistent with the statements that the disciples, after the resurrection, were regularly in the temple (Luke 24:53) and that they continued to meet in the temple precincts (Acts 2:46), Luke shows Peter and John going up to the temple "at the ninth hour, the hour of prayer," that is, at the time of the regular afternoon Tamid service (see Luke 1:10 and Acts 10:30), what we call 3 P.M.

Why Luke foregrounds this particular healing becomes evident when we attend to the details. What unfolds here interrupts routine. The friends of the beggar carry the immobile man and prop him up at the gate, a daily drill for them. And Peter and John are entering the temple precincts for their customary participation in the mid-afternoon liturgy (see Luke 24:53). When the beggar, apparently without looking, begs for alms (*eleēmosynē*), Peter commands him to look at them. Gaining his attention, he commands him to walk, using language that contrasts the power of

amazement toward them in the portico called "Solomon's Portico." [12]When Peter saw this, he addressed the people, "You Israelites, why are you amazed at this, and why do you look so intently at us as if we had made him walk by our own power or piety? [13]The God of Abraham, [the God] of Isaac, and [the God] of Jacob, the God of our ancestors, has glorified his servant Jesus whom you handed over and denied in Pilate's presence, when he had decided to release him. [14]You denied the Holy and Righteous One and asked that a murderer be released to you. [15]The author of life you put to death, but God raised him from the dead; of this we are witnesses. [16]And by faith in his name, this man, whom you see and know, his name has made strong, and the faith that comes through it has given him this perfect health, in the presence of all of you. [17]Now I know, brothers, that you acted out of ignorance, just as your leaders did; [18]but God has thus brought to fulfillment what he had announced beforehand through the mouth of all the prophets, that his Messiah would suffer. [19]Repent, therefore, and be converted, that your sins may be wiped away, [20]and that the Lord may grant you times of refreshment and send you the Messiah already appointed for you, Jesus, [21]whom heaven must receive until the times of universal restoration of which God spoke through the mouth

---

silver and gold with the power of the name of Jesus. Something astoundingly new breaks the routine of daily begging.

In the Greek Bible (the Septuagint, whose conventional sign is LXX), *eleēmosynē* sometimes means "alms," but more often it means "the mercy of God" (as in LXX Isa 1:27 and LXX Ps 23:5). The original readers of Luke's Greek would have been aware of a kind of pun here: the beggar was expecting *eleēmosynē* in the sense of mere alms; what he receives is a surprising *eleēmosynē*, the mercy of God in the form of liberation from lameness.

Luke emphasizes the fact that the man not only stands and walks—he *leaps*, a detail mentioned *twice* in verse 8. This stress on leaping recalls the only other place where the Bible mentions the lame leaping, Isaiah 35:6: "Then will the lame leap like a stag." Now it becomes clear why Luke chooses precisely this healing as the one to highlight in the context of his description of the birth of the church. Isaiah 35:5-6 is a prophetic description of the restoration of Israel, now understood as fulfilled in the Jerusalem messianic community.

Just as the Fourth Gospel, where faith in Jesus is the deepest kind of seeing and thus we are *all* born blind in that sense, highlights the healing of a man born *blind*, so Luke highlights this healing of a man born *lame*.

What the healing account itself began, with its allusion to Isaiah 35 in the language of leaping, the speech continues in its further interpretation of the healing, using still more references to the Scriptures.

of his holy prophets from of old. [22]For Moses said:

> 'A prophet like me will the Lord,
>   your God, raise up for you
>   from among your own kins-
>   men;
> to him you shall listen in all that he
>   may say to you.
> [23]Everyone who does not listen to
>   that prophet
> will be cut off from the
>   people.'

[24]Moreover, all the prophets who spoke, from Samuel and those afterwards, also announced these days. [25]You are the children of the prophets and of the covenant that God made with your ancestors when he said to Abraham, 'In your offspring all the families of the earth shall be blessed.' [26]For you first, God raised up his servant and sent him to bless you by turning each of you from your evil ways."

First, who did it? When the crowds attribute the healing to the apostles, Peter announces that this was the work of "the God of Abraham, of Isaac, and of Jacob," who has "glorified his servant Jesus." Since this way of referring to God echoes the call of Moses in Exodus 3:6, Peter may be implying that this healing is a sign that God is working a new Exodus through the long-awaited prophet-like-Moses, who is Jesus (recall the "wonders and signs" language of 2:19, 22).

This identification of Jesus is further underscored by the *pesher* citation of Deuteronomy 18:15, 18-19 at verses 22-23. Regarding the person who fails to respond to ("hear") God's words spoken by that prophet, Luke replaces Deuteronomy's vague warning ("I myself will make him answer for it") by substituting Leviticus's stiffer sanction for failing to participate in the liturgy of the Day of Atonement (Lev 23:29): "[that person] shall be cut off from his people." Notice that, as Luke understands it, Jews who accept Jesus as the Messiah do not divorce themselves from the people of Israel; rather, they constitute the true Israel, and those who fail to accept Jesus are, in effect, excommunicated.

This healing is also a sign of the end times: "*All* the prophets who spoke, from Samuel and those afterwards, also announced *these days*" (v. 24, emphasis added). Further, this healing is a sign that what is unfolding here in Jerusalem is a fulfillment of God's ancient promise to Abraham: "In your offspring all the families of the earth shall be blessed" (v. 25, alluding to Gen 22:18; and see 12:3; 26:4). In the final verse of the speech, Luke makes a clever play on the words "raise up" that were just heard in the quotation from Deuteronomy 18:15: God has indeed "raised up" his servant Jesus, not simply in the sense of commissioning him but also in the new sense of resurrection from the dead. Now the risen Lord is

4 ¹While they were still speaking to the people, the priests, the captain of the temple guard, and the Sadducees confronted them, ²disturbed that they were teaching the people and proclaiming in Jesus the resurrection of the dead. ³They laid hands on them and put them in custody until the next day, since it was already evening. ⁴But many of those who heard the word came to believe and [the] number of men grew to [about] five thousand.

Before the Sanhedrin. ⁵On the next day, their leaders, elders, and scribes were assembled in Jerusalem, ⁶with Annas the high priest, Caiaphas, John, Alexander, and all who were of the high-priestly class. ⁷They brought them into their presence and questioned them, "By what power or by what name have you done this?" ⁸Then Peter, filled with the holy Spirit, answered them, "Leaders of the people and elders: ⁹If we are being examined today about a good deed done to a cripple, namely, by what means he was saved, ¹⁰then all of you and all the people of Israel should know that it was in the name of Jesus Christ the Nazorean ▶

working through the likes of Peter and John, offering new opportunities for conversion to the life of the Spirit.

4:1-22 The temple authorities confront the apostles on the question of authority

The spectacle of Jesus' followers teaching crowds in the temple precincts ("Solomon's Portico," 3:11) alarms the temple authorities. Not only are these Galileans usurping their teaching authority with the people, they are proclaiming in Jesus "the resurrection of the dead," which, for the Sadducees, was one of the false doctrines of the Pharisees. The Sadducees held as true only what could be found in a strict reading of the Pentateuch (the first five books of the Old Testament), and they found no teaching about immortality or resurrection in those five scrolls (see Luke 20:27-40).

When the rulers and elders gather to meet as the Sanhedrin, they raise the same question they had earlier raised with Jesus after he had driven out the sellers and continued teaching daily in the temple area (Luke 20:1-8), namely, the question of authority. This time their question is about the power that healed the lame man: "By what power or by what name have you done this?" (v. 7). It is the same issue raised by the healing and addressed by Peter in the previous speech (3:12-13). And the answer is the same here. The healing was an act of God done in the name of Jesus; the healing showed that the Sanhedrin's judgment (Jesus was an offender deserving death) has been overruled by the "higher court" of God, as confirmed by the resurrection of Jesus.

whom you crucified, whom God raised from the dead; in his name this man stands before you healed. [11]He is 'the stone rejected by you, the builders, which has become the cornerstone.' [12]There is no salvation through anyone else, nor is there any other name under heaven given to the human race by which we are to be saved."

[13]Observing the boldness of Peter and John and perceiving them to be un-educated, ordinary men, they were amazed, and they recognized them as the companions of Jesus. [14]Then when they saw the man who had been cured standing there with them, they could say nothing in reply. [15]So they ordered them to leave the Sanhedrin, and conferred with one another, saying, [16]"What are we to do with these men? Everyone living in Jerusalem knows that a remarkable sign was done

Peter's empowerment by the holy Spirit fulfills Jesus' promise to his disciples in Luke 12:11-12. To drive home that this victory of God's power and authority is greater than any earthly authority, Peter cites a favorite psalm used by the church to celebrate God's action in the death and resurrection of Jesus (see Luke 20:17 and 1 Pet 2:7). Paraphrasing Psalm 118:22, Peter says to the assembly, "He is 'the stone rejected by you, the builders, which has become the cornerstone.'" In the context of Psalm 118, the rejected stone refers to Israel, cast aside by imperial power yet rescued by God, who will use it as a cornerstone. This verse serves wonderfully as a Christian *pesher* because it is not only an apt celebration of the death and resurrection of Jesus, but it also evokes the image of the end-time temple interpreted as the Christian community.

What is more, the theme of the psalm—that God's power to *save* is greater than imperial power—provides the background for Peter's word-play on the theme of healing/saving. The Greek word for "heal" and "save" in verses 9 and 12 is *sōzō*, which can mean any aspect of the whole range of rescuing, from physical healing to eschatological salvation. In verse 9 it denotes the physical healing of the paralytic, whereas in verse 12 it apparently refers to ultimate salvation. Thus the physical cure of the man born lame becomes not only a sign of the restoration of Israel but also of the full salvation of all who believe: "There is no *salvation* through anyone else, nor is there any other name under heaven given to the human race by which we are to be *saved*" (v. 12, emphasis added).

Although that verse is sometimes applied to the uniqueness of Jesus within the context of religious pluralism, a different context may be operating here. For an audience familiar with the claim of Roman emperors to the title of *sōtēr* ("Savior"), the mention of *sōtēria* ("salvation") suggests a contrast between the imperial power that controls the temple officials and

through them, and we cannot deny it. [17]But so that it may not be spread any further among the people, let us give them a stern warning never again to speak to anyone in this name."

[18]So they called them back and ordered them not to speak or teach at all in the name of Jesus. [19]Peter and John, however, said to them in reply, "Whether it is right in the sight of God for us to obey you rather than God, you be the judges. [20]It is impossible for us not to speak about what we have seen and heard." [21]After threatening them further, they released them, finding no way to punish them, on account of the people who were all praising God for what had happened. [22]For the man on whom this sign of healing had been done was over forty years old.

Prayer of the Community. [23]After their release they went back to their own people and reported what the chief priests and elders had told them. [24]And when they heard it, they raised their voices to God with one accord and said, "Sovereign Lord, maker of heaven and earth and the sea and all

the divine power working through Jesus. As in Psalm 118, true power and authority come not from worldly empire but from God's power, here exercised in the name of the risen Lord Jesus.

When the Sanhedrin orders the apostles "never again to speak to anyone in this name" (v. 17), Peter and John say, "Whether it is right in the sight of God for us to obey you rather than God, you be the judges." It is a clear assertion that these religious officials have lost whatever religious authority they had. The behavior of the Sanhedrin has shown that these men are more interested in preserving their own control than in serving the authority of God. That the healing of the beggar at the temple gate is "a remarkable sign" they readily admit, but they choose to ignore its significance. Luke underscores the public nature of this event in the closing statement in the episode: "For the man on whom this sign of healing had been done was over forty years old" (and therefore well known to frequenters of the Temple Mount).

4:23-31 The prayer of the community and God's response

Luke portrays Peter and John returning and reporting to "their own" (Luke could mean anything from the Twelve, to the 120 of Acts 1:15, to the 5000 "men" [*andres*] mentioned at 4:4) what the chief priests and elders had told them. What follows is either (a) a miracle of choral speaking, in which this large group improvises a *pesher* interpretation in unison or (b) a prayer-speech that historian Luke composes (in *pesher* style) to convey how the early community understood persecution and responded to it in their prayer and action. The latter seems more likely.

that is in them, [25]you said by the holy Spirit through the mouth of our father David, your servant:

> 'Why did the Gentiles rage
> and the peoples entertain folly?
> [26]The kings of the earth took their stand
> and the princes gathered together
> against the Lord and against his anointed.'

[27]Indeed they gathered in this city against your holy servant Jesus whom you anointed, Herod and Pontius Pilate, together with the Gentiles and the peoples of Israel, [28]to do what your hand and [your] will had long ago planned to take place. [29]And now, Lord, take note of their threats, and enable your servants to speak your word with all boldness, [30]as you stretch forth [your] hand to heal, and signs and

---

This episode presents us with one of the most striking examples of *pesher* interpretation in the entire New Testament. Luke introduces it by having the group invoke God as creator (v. 24b: "Sovereign Lord, maker of heaven and earth and the sea and all that is in them"). Then they quote the first two verses of Psalm 2. The community then proceeds to apply the references to persons and actions of the initial verses in Psalm 2 to the actors and happenings of their recent experience in Jerusalem. "The Gentiles" are of course the Romans. "The peoples"—in the context of the psalm, a parallel expression for the Gentiles—now becomes "the peoples of Israel" (note that Luke retains the plural, "peoples," to echo the wording of the psalm). As for "the kings of the earth," Herod Antipas was the king before whom Jesus was arraigned (see Luke 23:6-12), and Pilate was the representative of the "king" of the Roman Empire. The "rulers" are the Sanhedrin leaders (see vv. 5 and 8) who had also just forbidden them to speak any more about Jesus. And they had indeed "gathered in this city against your holy servant Jesus whom God had *anointed*" ("christed" catches the overtones of the Greek).

When we hear "And now, Lord, take note of their threats" (v. 29), knowing the thrust of the rest of Psalm 2, we might expect something like "shatter them like an earthen dish" (Ps 2:9b). Instead, we hear quite the opposite: "Enable your servants to speak your word with all boldness, as you stretch forth [your] hand to heal, and signs and wonders are done through the name of your holy servant Jesus" (vv. 29-30). In response to the official crucifixion of Jesus and the present resistance of the rulers, they pray for empowerment to continue the mission of Jesus in word and work, especially preaching and healing. The divine response to their prayer (v. 31) is the "mini-Pentecost" that follows.

wonders are done through the name of your holy servant Jesus." [31]As they prayed, the place where they were gathered shook, and they were all filled with the holy Spirit and continued to speak the word of God with boldness.

Life in the Christian Community. [32]The community of believers was of one heart and mind, and no one claimed that any of his possessions was his own, but they had everything in common. [33]With great power the apostles bore witness to the resurrection of the Lord Jesus, and great favor was accorded them all. [34]There was no needy person among them, for those who owned property or houses would sell them, bring the proceeds of the sale, [35]and put them at the feet of the apostles, and they were distributed to each according to need.

[36]Thus Joseph, also named by the apostles Barnabas (which is translated "son of encouragement"), a Levite, a Cypriot by birth, [37]sold a piece of property that he owned, then brought the money and put it at the feet of the apostles.

5 Ananias and Sapphira. [1]A man named Ananias, however, with his wife Sapphira, sold a piece of property. [2]He retained for himself, with his wife's knowledge, some of the purchase price, took the remainder, and put it at the feet of the apostles. [3]But Peter said, "Ananias, why has Satan filled your heart so that you lied to the holy Spirit and retained part of the price of the land? [4]While it remained unsold, did it not remain yours? And when it was sold, was it not still under your control? Why did you contrive this deed?

4:32–5:11 Life in the Christian community

Acts 4:32-35 provides another cameo picture of the Jerusalem Christian community. With Acts 2:42-47, it makes a frame around the intervening episodes, which exemplify how God has worked through the leadership of the apostles (Peter and John) to continue Jesus' preaching and healing ministry. The description of the community as being "of one heart and mind" and holding everything in common embodies the Greek ideal of friendship. And the statement that "there was no needy person among them" alludes to the Hebrew ideal of covenant justice expressed in Deuteronomy 15:4. The jubilee note struck here echoes the jubilee theme of the passage from Isaiah 61 that Jesus read at his debut in the Nazareth synagogue (Luke 4:18-19). This spontaneous "faith sharing" of material goods to meet the needs of all is mediated through the leadership, a fact that is signified by their laying the proceeds of real estate sales "at the feet of the apostles" (v. 37).

To show that even from the beginning it was a struggle to live out the ideals of Christian community life, Luke now presents examples. First he offers a good example in Joseph Barnabas, who did it right (4:36-37). Then

You have lied not to human beings, but to God." ⁵When Ananias heard these words, he fell down and breathed his last, and great fear came upon all who heard of it. ⁶The young men came and wrapped him up, then carried him out and buried him.

⁷After an interval of about three hours, his wife came in, unaware of what had happened. ⁸Peter said to her, "Tell me, did you sell the land for this amount?" She answered, "Yes, for that amount." ⁹Then Peter said to her, "Why did you agree to test the Spirit of the Lord? Listen, the footsteps of those who have buried your husband are at the door, and they will carry you out." ¹⁰At once, she fell down at his feet and breathed her last. When the young men entered they found her dead, so they carried her out and buried her beside her husband. ¹¹And great fear came upon the whole church and upon all who heard of these things.

Signs and Wonders of the Apostles. ¹²Many signs and wonders were done among the people at the hands of the apostles. They were all together in Solomon's portico. ¹³None of the others dared to join them, but the people esteemed them. ¹⁴Yet more than ever, believers in the Lord, great numbers of men and women, were added to them. ¹⁵Thus they even carried the sick out into the streets and laid them on cots and mats so that when Peter came by, at least his shadow might fall on one or another of them. ¹⁶A large number of

---

comes a dramatic account of a bad example, the deceptive behavior of Ananias and Sapphira (5:1-11).

The reference to Barnabas introduces one who will emerge as a key player in the Jerusalem Christian community and its mission. (So important does this coworker of Paul become that the second-century *Epistle of Barnabas* was attributed to him.)

The sin of Ananias and Sapphira lies not so much in possessiveness as in their deception. As Peter himself grants, the property was theirs to keep or sell as they wished. But pretending that they were donating the whole proceeds, when in fact they were holding back part—this was nothing less than lying to the holy Spirit! Ironically, Luke notes that Sapphira falls dead "at the feet" of Peter as punishment for deceptively laying "at the feet of the apostles" only part of the property proceeds from the sale of their property. What is done to the community is done to the Spirit of God. The whole episode echoes another famous holding back, that of Achan, who, after the battle of Jericho, kept for himself some of the banned goods (Josh 7).

5:12-16 Another summary

The Jesus group continues to assemble in the temple precincts (see 3:11). And the "signs and wonders" that God had done through Jesus

people from the towns in the vicinity of Jerusalem also gathered, bringing the sick and those disturbed by unclean spirits, and they were all cured.

Trial before the Sanhedrin. [17]Then the high priest rose up and all his companions, that is, the party of the Sadducees, and, filled with jealousy, [18]laid hands upon the apostles and put them in the public jail. [19]But during the night, the angel of the Lord opened the doors of the prison, led them out, and said, [20]"Go and take your place in the temple area, and tell the people everything about this life." [21]When they heard this, they went to the temple early in the morning and taught. When the high priest and his companions arrived, they convened the Sanhedrin, the full senate of the Israelites, and sent to the jail to have them brought in. [22]But the court officers who went did not find them in the prison, so they came back and reported, [23]"We found the jail securely locked and the guards stationed outside the doors, but when we opened them, we found no one inside." [24]When they heard this report, the captain of the temple guard and the chief priests were at a loss about them, as to what this would come to. [25]Then someone came in and reported to them, "The men whom you put in prison are in the temple area and are teaching the people." [26]Then the captain and the court officers went and brought them in, but without force, because they were afraid of being stoned by the people.

[27]When they had brought them in and made them stand before the Sanhedrin, the high priest questioned them, [28]"We gave you strict orders [did we not?] to stop teaching in that name. Yet you have filled Jerusalem with your teaching and want to bring this man's blood upon us." [29]But Peter and the apostles said in reply, "We must obey God rather than men. [30]The God of our ancestors raised Jesus, though you had him killed by hanging him on a tree. [31]God exalted him at his right hand as leader and savior to grant Israel repentance and forgiveness of sins. [32]We are witnesses of these things, as is the holy Spirit that God has given to those who obey him."

[33]When they heard this, they became infuriated and wanted to put them to death. [34]But a Pharisee in the

---

(2:22), for the continuation of which they had prayed (4:30), continue to happen through the apostles. As contact with the mere tassel of Jesus' garment was enough to occasion healing in his ministry (Luke 8:43-44), now people seek even Peter's passing shadow as a medium of healing and deliverance from evil spirits.

5:17-42 Testing the mission: the work of God or human beings?

With divine help, the apostles move from prison to preaching. Strikingly, when the angel of the Lord opens the prison gates for them, he instructs them to go and take their stand in the temple and tell the people all about "this life." Like their Master, who entered the temple not simply to

Sanhedrin named Gamaliel, a teacher of the law, respected by all the people, stood up, ordered the men to be put outside for a short time, ³⁵and said to them, "Fellow Israelites, be careful what you are about to do to these men. ³⁶Some time ago, Theudas appeared, claiming to be someone important, and about four hundred men joined him, but he was killed, and all those who were loyal to him were disbanded and came to nothing. ³⁷After him came Judas the Galilean at the time of the census. He also drew people after him, but he too perished and all who were loyal to him were scattered. ³⁸So now I tell you, have nothing to do with these men, and let them go. For if this endeavor or this activity is of human origin, it will destroy itself. ³⁹But if it comes from God, you will not be able to destroy them; you may even find yourselves fighting against God." They were persuaded by him. ⁴⁰After recalling the apostles, they had them flogged, ordered them to stop speaking in the name of Jesus, and dismissed them. ⁴¹So they left the presence of the Sanhedrin, rejoicing that they had been found worthy to suffer dishonor for the

---

expel the vendors but also to take his stand there and teach the people daily (Luke 19:45–21:38; and see Luke 2:46, where the twelve-year-old Jesus teaches in the temple), the apostles, too, continue the mission in what remains for them their sacred center, the temple area. Like Jesus, they *occupy* the temple precincts as the right place to do God's will by teaching the people (5:21, 42; see Luke 20:1).

This miraculous "jail break" strikes the theme of the unhindered word that will be reprised in the great escape of Acts 12. Indeed, the final word of the book is *akōlytōs* ("without hindrance"), describing Paul's preaching the kingdom of God and the Lord Jesus Christ even while under house arrest (28:31).

When they are accused of disobeying orders, Peter and the apostles repeat what Peter and John had said once before to the Sanhedrin, namely, that when divine and human orders collide, they must obey God rather than human beings (v. 29; see 4:19-20). To justify this response, they cite the ruling of a "higher court." Drawing upon what will become a traditional Christian application of Scripture, they announce that in the resurrection God has overruled the curse of crucifixion (death by "hanging . . . on a tree"; see Deut 21:23 and Gal 3:13) by exalting Jesus to his "right hand" (Ps 110:1). And the purpose of this is to renew the people of God, Israel.

Then comes the famous intervention of Rabbi Gamaliel, whom Paul will name as his mentor in Acts 22:3. Citing the short-lived movements of other would-be messiahs—Theudas and Judas the Galilean—Gamaliel argues that obedience to false prophets comes to nothing; so let (divinely

sake of the name. [42]And all day long, both at the temple and in their homes, they did not stop teaching and proclaiming the Messiah, Jesus.

6 **The Need for Assistants.** [1]At that time, as the number of disciples continued to grow, the Hellenists complained against the Hebrews because their widows were being neglected in the daily distribution. [2]So the Twelve called together the community of the disciples and said, "It is not right for us to neglect the word of God to serve at table. [3]Brothers, select from among you seven reputable men, filled with the Spirit and wisdom, whom we shall appoint to this task, [4]whereas we shall devote ourselves to prayer and to the ministry of the word." [5]The proposal was acceptable to the whole community, so they chose Stephen, a man filled with faith and the holy Spirit, also Philip, Prochorus, Nicanor, Timon, Parmenas, and Nicholas of Antioch, a convert to Judaism. [6]They presented these ▶ men to the apostles who prayed and laid hands on them. [7]The word of God ▶ continued to spread, and the number of

guided) history show whether this Jesus movement is of God or not. The implication is that Jesus will be shown to be another false prophet. The Sanhedrin chooses to listen to a man, Gamaliel, rather than to the evidence of God demonstrated in the signs and wonders done through the apostles. At the same time, Gamaliel's wait-and-see approach exemplifies the kind of openness that led to others of the house of Israel eventually accepting Jesus as their Messiah.

Acts 6:1-7 Crisis and solution: choosing the Seven

No sooner had the Jerusalem church dealt with challenges from the outside than it had to deal with an internal conflict—a quarrel between "Hellenists" and "Hebrews" regarding an alleged neglect of the widows among the Hellenists. The "Hellenists" are best understood as Greek-speaking Jews, probably people who grew up in the Diaspora (Jewish communities scattered outside Palestine beginning after the Babylonian Exile) and later immigrated to Judea. "Hebrews," then, would be indigenous, Aramaic-speaking Jews. We have evidence, even as far back as the Maccabees (ca. 170 B.C.), that there had long been tension between the Jews who had taken on the language and even some of the customs of the Hellenistic world, on the one hand, and the more traditional Jews who preferred to speak Aramaic and avoid Hellenistic ways, on the other. This passage lets us know that the infant Christian community of Jerusalem included Jews from both subgroups and that becoming Christian did not automatically remove the "liberal" or "conservative" baggage that they brought with them.

the disciples in Jerusalem increased greatly; even a large group of priests were becoming obedient to the faith.

Accusation against Stephen. [8]Now Stephen, filled with grace and power, was working great wonders and signs among the people. [9]Certain members of the so-called Synagogue of Freedmen, Cyrenians, and Alexandrians, and people from Cilicia and Asia, came forward and debated with Stephen, [10]but they could not withstand the wisdom and the spirit with which he spoke. [11]Then they instigated some men to say, "We have heard him speaking blasphemous words against Moses and God." [12]They stirred up the people, the elders, and the scribes, accosted him, seized him, and brought him before the Sanhedrin. [13]They presented false witnesses who testified, "This man never stops saying things against [this] holy place and the law. [14]For we have heard him claim that this Jesus the Nazorean

---

Luke informs us that the community had set up a daily dole (of food, presumably) to take care of the needy among them, especially widows. But the widows of the Greek-speaking group were somehow being neglected. Luke does not mention the cause of the neglect. (Was it a combination of scarcity and prejudice—the ["Hebrew"] Twelve favoring their own kind? Or were they too busy to oversee the distribution properly?) Whatever the source of the problem, the Twelve apply a familiar practical solution: they increase the staff. Too busy with the service (*diakonia*) of the word to tie up their time with serving at table, they call the entire community together (here called "disciples" for the first time in Acts) and charge them to select seven good men to carry out this other *diakonia*. That the seven chosen all have Greek names suggests a kind of affirmative action on the part of the community: they choose members of the Greek-speaking group, thereby assuring that the neglect of the Hellenists' widows would be remedied.

Although the word for the service (of both word and table) is *diakonia*, the Seven are not called *diakonoi* (from which comes the English word "deacons"). Moreover, the service performed by Martha (Luke 10:40), the Twelve (Acts 1:12, 25), and Peter and Silas (12:25) is also termed *diakonia*, indicating that the term has not yet acquired its technical sense. Still, although Luke is probably not describing the creation of the office of deacon here, this episode points toward the later three-tier structure of bishop-priests-deacons reflected in the writing of Ignatius of Antioch. For that reason, this passage has traditionally been associated with the church office of deacon.

This freeing up of the Twelve leads to a continuing rapid growth of the church, even attracting some of the temple priests to the fold.

will destroy this place and change the customs that Moses handed down to us." [15]All those who sat in the Sanhedrin looked intently at him and saw that his face was like the face of an angel.

7 **Stephen's Discourses.** [1]Then the high priest asked, "Is this so?" [2]And he replied, "My brothers and fathers, listen. The God of glory appeared to our father Abraham while he was in Mesopotamia, before he had settled in Haran, [3]and said to him, 'Go forth from your land and [from] your kinsfolk to the land that I will show you.' [4]So he went forth from the land of the Chaldeans and settled in Haran. And from there, after his father died, he made him migrate to this land where you now dwell. [5]Yet he gave him no inheritance in it, not even a foot's length, but he did promise to give it to him and

---

6:8-15 Stephen accused

Curiously, after Stephen has been commissioned as one of the Seven to "serve at table," thereby freeing the apostles for the service of the word, Luke proceeds to show Stephen engaged in precisely that apostolic work. Like the Twelve (2:43; 4:30; 5:12) and like Jesus before them (2:22), he is filled with power to do "wonders and signs" (6:8). What Luke describes is more a matter of prophetic succession than delegation: Jesus to the Twelve, then the Twelve to the Seven, exemplified by Stephen. Luke will indicate in Stephen's speech that the line of succession reaches back to Moses and the patriarchs, even as it reaches forward to the church of Luke's day (and ours). The same Spirit that empowered Jesus and the Twelve to preach and heal empowers Stephen to do the same.

As in the case of Jesus and the Twelve, the exercise of that prophetic ministry meets opposition, arrest, and a hasty "trial." Whereas Luke had omitted any mention of false witnesses in his very brief account of the Sanhedrin's investigation of Jesus (Luke 22:66-71), as he also omits in his presentation of the crucifixion Mark's taunt of the head-wagging passersby about destroying and building the temple, he does introduce here some false witness against Stephen. Like the witnesses at the trial of Jesus in Mark and Matthew, they accuse their adversary of threatening the holy place (the temple). They also make him out to be an enemy of the Law of Moses. The discourse that follows in the next chapter will do much more than simply rebut those charges. It will show how the Law and the temple reach fulfillment in Christian life and worship.

7:1-53 Stephen addresses the Sanhedrin

In Luke's Gospel the risen Jesus spoke to his disciples about the fulfillment of things written about him in the Law of Moses, the prophets, and

his descendants as a possession, even though he was childless. ⁶And God spoke thus, 'His descendants shall be aliens in a land not their own, where they shall be enslaved and oppressed for four hundred years; ⁷but I will bring judgment on the nation they serve,' God said, 'and after that they will come out and worship me in this place.' ⁸Then he gave him the covenant of circumcision, and so he became the father of Isaac, and circumcised him on the eighth day, as Isaac did Jacob, and Jacob the twelve patriarchs

⁹"And the patriarchs, jealous of Joseph, sold him into slavery in Egypt; but God was with him ¹⁰and rescued him from all his afflictions. He granted him favor and wisdom before Pharaoh, the king of Egypt, who put him in charge of Egypt and [of] his entire household. ¹¹Then a famine and great affliction struck all Egypt and Canaan, and our ancestors could find no food; ¹²but when Jacob heard that there was grain in Egypt, he sent our ancestors there a first time. ¹³The second time, Joseph made himself known to his brothers, and Joseph's family became known to Pharaoh. ¹⁴Then Joseph sent for his father Jacob, inviting him and his whole clan, seventy-five persons; ¹⁵and Jacob went down to Egypt. And he and our ancestors died ¹⁶and were brought back to Shechem and placed in the tomb that Abraham had purchased for a sum of money from the sons of Hamor at Shechem.

---

the psalms (Luke 24:27, 44). Our author has already shown us how the events of Jesus' life, especially his death and resurrection (Luke 24:46), fulfill the Law of Moses (the Torah, or first five books of the Bible). Peter's speech in Acts 3:22 gave one example: Jesus is the prophet-like-Moses whom God would "raise up," alluding to Deuteronomy 18:15.

Now, in the first half of Stephen's speech, the longest speech in Acts (more than twice as long as Peter's Pentecost speech), we hear Torah narrative applied to Jesus at length. Without explicitly mentioning the name of Jesus Messiah—"the righteous one" at verse 52 being as close as he comes—Stephen retells the stories of Abraham, Joseph, and Moses in ways that point to Jesus' death and resurrection and to the post-Easter church.

Just as the canticles of Mary and Zechariah celebrated the conception of Jesus and the birth of John the Baptist as leading to the fulfillment of God's promises to Abraham (Luke 2:55 and 73), Stephen tells of God's promise to Abraham that he would give the land to his descendents through a process that would entail rescue from slavery "in a land not their own" (v. 6) to freedom to "worship me in this place" (v. 7). In that last phrase Luke alludes to God's promise to *Moses* regarding worship at *Sinai* (Exod 3:12) and makes *this place* refer to *Jerusalem*. The remainder of Acts will portray true worship centered on the risen Jesus (recall that the disciples had worshiped the risen Lord on Easter Sunday near Bethany, Luke 24:52).

¹⁷"When the time drew near for the fulfillment of the promise that God pledged to Abraham, the people had increased and become very numerous in Egypt, ¹⁸until another king who knew nothing of Joseph came to power [in Egypt]. ¹⁹He dealt shrewdly with our people and oppressed [our] ancestors by forcing them to expose their infants, that they might not survive. ²⁰At this time Moses was born, and he was extremely beautiful. For three months he was nursed in his father's house; ²¹but when he was exposed, Pharaoh's daughter adopted him and brought him up as her own son. ²²Moses was educated [in] all the wisdom of the Egyptians and was powerful in his words and deeds.

²³"When he was forty years old, he decided to visit his kinsfolk, the Israel-ites. ²⁴When he saw one of them treated unjustly, he defended and avenged the oppressed man by striking down the Egyptian. ²⁵He assumed [his] kinsfolk would understand that God was offering them deliverance through him, but they did not understand. ²⁶The next day he appeared to them as they were fighting and tried to reconcile them peacefully, saying, 'Men, you are brothers. Why are you harming one another?' ²⁷Then the one who was harming his neighbor pushed him aside, saying, 'Who appointed you ruler and judge over us? ²⁸Are you thinking of killing me as you killed the Egyptian yesterday?' ²⁹Moses fled when he heard this and settled as an alien in the land of Midian, where he became the father of two sons.

³⁰"Forty years later, an angel appeared to him in the desert near Mount

---

The brief account of the Joseph story then serves to illustrate how God begins to fulfill the promises to Abraham by rescuing his descendants from famine by means of a person who was first rejected and later emerges as their savior. The brother they had sold to slave traders eventually rose to become a prime minister whose grain reserve program saved their lives.

This pattern of God working through a rejected-one-become-savior is elaborated more fully in the rendition of the story of Moses that follows. And here Luke chooses words even more carefully to highlight the parallels between Moses and Jesus. The young Moses was "powerful in his words and deeds" (v. 22; see Luke 24:19 regarding Jesus). Like Jesus, Moses was misunderstood by his kin (v. 25). As Moses was asked, "Who appointed you ruler and judge over us?" (v. 27), so too was Jesus (Luke 12:14). Luke then becomes more richly specific in verses 35-36: "This Moses whom they had rejected . . . God sent as [both] ruler and deliverer. . . . This man led them out, performing *wonders and signs* in the land of Egypt, at the Red Sea, and in the desert for forty years" (emphasis

Sinai in the flame of a burning bush. ³¹When Moses saw it, he was amazed at the sight, and as he drew near to look at it, the voice of the Lord came, ³²'I am the God of your fathers, the God of Abraham, of Isaac, and of Jacob.' Then Moses, trembling, did not dare to look at it. ³³But the Lord said to him, 'Remove the sandals from your feet, for the place where you stand is holy ground. ³⁴I have witnessed the affliction of my people in Egypt and have heard their groaning, and I have come down to rescue them. Come now, I will send you to Egypt.' ³⁵This Moses, whom they had rejected with the words, 'Who appointed you ruler and judge?' God sent as [both] ruler and deliverer, through the angel who appeared to him in the bush. ³⁶This man led them out, performing wonders and signs in the land of Egypt, at the Red Sea, and in the desert for forty years. ³⁷It was this Moses who said to the Israelites, 'God will raise up for you, from among your own kinsfolk, a prophet like me.' ³⁸It was he who, in the assembly in the desert, was with the angel who spoke to him on Mount Sinai and with our ancestors, and he received living utterances to hand on to us.

³⁹"Our ancestors were unwilling to obey him; instead, they pushed him aside and in their hearts turned back to Egypt, ⁴⁰saying to Aaron, 'Make us gods who will be our leaders. As for that Moses who led us out of the land of Egypt, we do not know what has happened to him.' ⁴¹So they made a calf in those days, offered sacrifice to the idol, and reveled in the works of their hands. ⁴²Then God turned and handed

---

added). Note how Acts uses the phrase "wonders and signs," first found in the quotation of Joel in Acts 2:19, both for what God did through Jesus (Acts 2:22) and for what God now does through the apostles (2:43; 4:30).

If readers have not grasped the connection with Jesus by this time, our author makes it crystal-clear with the reference to Deuteronomy 18:15 at verse 37: "God will raise up for you, from among your own kinsfolk, a prophet like me." That this applies to Jesus was already established in Peter's speech (Acts 3:22).

Thus far Stephen has dealt with the charge that he speaks against the Law; indeed, he has shown how the message about Jesus fulfills the thrust of the narratives about the ancestors and Moses. Now the speech takes up the matter of the temple, which this discourse takes to be really a question of what makes for true worship. If God promised Abraham that Israel would come to "worship . . . in this place" (v. 7), how has that promise been fulfilled? Stephen says that the people have been disobedient in the matter of worship from the beginning. First there was the idolatry of the golden calf (vv. 39-41). Then God gave them over to worship of the gods of the nations, as exemplified in the Greek version of Amos 5:25, which

them over to worship the host of heaven, as it is written in the book of the prophets:

> 'Did you bring me sacrifices and
>   offerings
>   for forty years in the desert, O
>   house of Israel?
> [43]No, you took up the tent of
>   Moloch
> and the star of [your] god
>   Rephan,
>   the images that you made to
>   worship.
> So I shall take you into exile beyond
>   Babylon.'

[44]"Our ancestors had the tent of testimony in the desert just as the One who spoke to Moses directed him to make it according to the pattern he had seen. [45]Our ancestors who inherited it brought it with Joshua when they dispossessed the nations that God drove out from before our ancestors, up to the time of David, [46]who found favor in the sight of God and asked that he might find a dwelling place for the house of Jacob. [47]But Solomon built a house for him. [48]Yet the Most High does not dwell in houses made by human hands. As the prophet says:

> [49]'The heavens are my throne,
>   the earth is my footstool.
> What kind of house can you build
>   for me?
>   says the Lord,
>   or what is to be my resting
>   place?
> [50]Did not my hand make all these
>   things?'

Conclusion. [51]"You stiff-necked people, uncircumcised in heart and ears, you always oppose the holy Spirit; you are just like your ancestors. [52]Which of the prophets did your ancestors not persecute? They put to death those who foretold the coming of ▶

Luke applies to the whole period before their exile in Babylon by changing Amos's reference to exile beyond Damascus to exile beyond Babylon. The speech makes the case that the move beyond the divinely mandated portable tent of testimony (the desert tabernacle, the place of the divine presence) to the fixed and solid temple built by Solomon was misunderstood by some in Israel as a way of magically confining God to that space. That misunderstanding was a step in the direction of idolatry and an attempt to box God, who "does not *dwell* in houses made by human hands," as illustrated by the quotation from Isaiah 66:1-2 (emphasis added).

By this time in the speech, Stephen has moved from a story about "*our* ancestors" (v. 39) to one about "*your* ancestors" (v. 52, emphasis added). His climactic word to those who have accused him of speaking against the Law is to accuse them of not observing it themselves.

7:54-60 The martyrdom of Stephen

If the charges brought against Stephen had suggested a parallel with the synoptic tradition of the trial of Jesus, the death of Stephen clearly and powerfully mirrors the death of Jesus—and also responds to the question

the righteous one, whose betrayers and murderers you have now become. ⁵³You received the law as transmitted by angels, but you did not observe it."

Stephen's Martyrdom. ⁵⁴When they heard this, they were infuriated, and they ground their teeth at him. ⁵⁵But he, filled with the holy Spirit, looked up intently to heaven and saw the glory of God and Jesus standing at the right hand of God, ⁵⁶and he said, "Behold, I see the heavens opened and the Son of Man standing at the right hand of God." ⁵⁷But they cried out in a loud voice, covered their ears, and rushed upon him together. ⁵⁸They threw him out of the city, and began to stone him. The witnesses laid down their cloaks at the feet of a young man named Saul. ⁵⁹As they were stoning Stephen, he called out, "Lord Jesus, receive my spirit." ⁶⁰Then he fell to his knees and cried out in a loud voice, "Lord, do not hold this sin against them"; and when he said this, he fell asleep.

8 ¹Now Saul was consenting to his execution.

Persecution of the Church. On that day, there broke out a severe persecution of the church in Jerusalem, and all were scattered throughout the countryside of Judea and Samaria, except the apostles. ²Devout men buried Stephen and made a loud lament over him. ³Saul, meanwhile, was trying to destroy the church; entering house after house and dragging out men and women, he handed them over for imprisonment.

III. The Mission in Judea and Samaria

Philip in Samaria. ⁴Now those who had been scattered went about preaching the word. ⁵Thus Philip went down of true worship. When Stephen announces a vision of the heavens opening and the Son of Man standing at the right hand of God (v. 56), his adversaries take him outside of the city to kill him, just as they did to his Master. And just as Jesus commended his spirit to the Father, Stephen can pray, "Lord Jesus, receive my spirit" (v. 59; see Luke 23:46). As Jesus prayed to God to forgive his crucifiers, so Stephen prays to *Jesus*, "Lord, do not hold this sin against them" (v. 60).

Two themes shine through this narrative: (1) the follower of Jesus relives the story of Jesus, sometimes quite literally; (2) Stephen answers the question about true worship with his prayer to Jesus as Lord and with the giving up of his life.

8:1-3 Saul (Paul) spearheads the persecution of the church

Saul, first mentioned as minding the cloaks of Stephen's stoners at 7:58, is said to approve this extra-judicial execution (8:1), which triggers a persecution of the church in Jerusalem. Thus begins a scattering of "Jews for Jesus" throughout Judea and Samaria. The note that the apostles were exempt from the persecution suggests that it was the Hellenists who are scattered.

to [the] city of Samaria and proclaimed the Messiah to them. ⁶With one accord, the crowds paid attention to what was said by Philip when they heard it and saw the signs he was doing. ⁷For unclean spirits, crying out in a loud voice, came out of many possessed people, and many paralyzed and crippled people were cured. ⁸There was great joy in that city.

Simon the Magician. ⁹A man named Simon used to practice magic in the city and astounded the people of Samaria, claiming to be someone great. ¹⁰All of them, from the least to the greatest, paid attention to him, saying, "This man is the 'Power of God' that is called 'Great.'" ¹¹They paid attention to him because he had astounded them by his magic for a long time, ¹²but once they began to believe Philip as he preached the good news about the kingdom of God and the name of Jesus Christ, men and women alike were baptized. ¹³Even Simon himself believed and, after being baptized, became devoted to Philip; and when he saw the signs and mighty deeds that were occurring, he was astounded.

¹⁴Now when the apostles in Jerusalem heard that Samaria had accepted the word of God, they sent them Peter and John, ¹⁵who went down and prayed

THE MISSION IN JUDEA AND SAMARIA

Acts 8:4–9:43

In the remainder of chapter 8 and all of chapter 9, Luke presents Philip evangelizing the margins of Israel among the Samaritans and with the Ethiopian eunuch. Then comes the conversion/call of Saul on the road to Damascus and, finally, Peter's work among his fellow Jews, just before his dramatic experience with Cornelius's household draws him into mission to the Gentiles. In germ, these two chapters describe the major transitions announced in Acts 1:8: "You will be my witnesses in Jerusalem, throughout Judea and Samaria, and to the ends of the earth." Philip, Saul (Paul), and Peter take the last three steps.

8:4-25 Philip the evangelist versus Simon the magician

We saw that Stephen was a mouthpiece for Lukan Christology (the doctrines of the person and works of Christ) and also an example of the imitation of Christ. Now another member of the Seven, Philip, enters the scene as another kind of example. The first episode featuring Philip demonstrates how the Christian mission extends beyond Judea into the realm of the "heretical" (from the Jewish point of view) Samaritans and how that mission trumps the pagan magic typified by Simon Magus.

To describe the outreach of the mission beyond Jerusalem to the margins of the people of Israel, Luke five times uses his favorite word for that—

for them, that they might receive the holy Spirit, [16]for it had not yet fallen upon any of them; they had only been baptized in the name of the Lord Jesus. [17]Then they laid hands on them and they received the holy Spirit.

[18]When Simon saw that the Spirit was conferred by the laying on of the apostles' hands, he offered them money [19]and said, "Give me this power too, so that anyone upon whom I lay my hands may receive the holy Spirit." [20]But Peter said to him, "May your money perish with you, because you thought that you could buy the gift of God with money. [21]You have no share or lot in this matter, for your heart is not upright before God. [22]Repent of this wickedness of yours and pray to the Lord that, if possible, your intention may be forgiven. [23]For I see that you are filled with bitter gall and are in the bonds of iniquity." [24]Simon said in reply, "Pray for me to the Lord, that nothing of what you have said may come upon me." [25]So when they had testified and proclaimed the word of the Lord, they returned to Jerusalem and preached the good news to many Samaritan villages.

---

euangelizomai, from which we get our word "evangelize." Luke found it in his Greek Bible, especially in Isaiah (40:9; 52:7; 60:6; 61:1), where the prophet speaks of announcing the coming saving power of God. Luke employs the word to describe the preaching of angels (Luke 1:19; 2:10), of John the Baptist (3:18), of Jesus (4:18 [Isa 61:1]; 4:43; 7:22; 8:1; 9:6; 16:16; 20:1), of the apostles (Acts 5:42); and in the present episode, the word describes the mission of the whole dispersed church (8:4), of Philip (vv. 12, 35, 40), and of Peter and John (v. 25). It is all a matter of telling what God is doing.

After describing the preaching and healing of Philip in words that recall the work of Jesus and the apostles (8:7), Luke speaks of the conversion of one Simon. Though he had gained an enthusiastic following as a magician before Philip's arrival, even he is converted by Philip's evangelizing (vv. 9-13). (Our word "simony," denoting the purchase or sale of spiritual things, derives from Simon Magus, alluding to his misguided attempt to buy the power to mediate the holy Spirit [vv. 18-19].)

Curiously, only when the apostles Peter and John come down from Jerusalem to pray for and lay hands on the Samaritan converts do they receive the holy Spirit (vv. 14-17). Luke here distinguishes between baptism "in the name of the Lord Jesus" and this infusion of the Spirit. A similar distinction will be made later—but in reversed order (Spirit baptism, then baptism in the name of Jesus)—in the conversion of Cornelius and his household (10:44-49).

Though some Christian groups have turned this narrative distinction into a doctrine of two baptisms (water baptism and Spirit baptism), Luke,

Philip and the Ethiopian. ²⁶Then the angel of the Lord spoke to Philip, "Get up and head south on the road that goes down from Jerusalem to Gaza, the desert route." ²⁷So he got up and set out. Now there was an Ethiopian eunuch, a court official of the Candace, that is, the queen of the Ethiopians, in charge of her entire treasury, who had come to Jerusalem to worship, ²⁸and was returning home. Seated in his chariot, he was reading the prophet Isaiah. ²⁹The Spirit said to Philip, "Go and join up with that chariot." ³⁰Philip ran up and heard him reading Isaiah the prophet and said, "Do you understand what you are reading?" ³¹He replied, "How can I, unless someone instructs me?" So he invited Philip to get in and sit with him. ³²This was the scripture passage he was reading:

"Like a sheep he was led to the
    slaughter,
  and as a lamb before its shearer
    is silent,
    so he opened not his mouth.
³³In [his] humiliation justice was
    denied him.
  Who will tell of his posterity?
    For his life is taken from the
    earth."

³⁴Then the eunuch said to Philip in reply, "I beg you, about whom is the prophet saying this? About himself, or

---

followed by the Catholic tradition, presents as normative Peter's description of baptism and reception of the holy Spirit as one unified event (2:38). Where Luke narratively separates Spirit and baptism, he seems to be making a special point in each case. Here the point is to underscore the privileged role the apostles have in affirming the mission to the Samaritans through their mediation of the Spirit.

8:26-40 Philip and the Ethiopian eunuch

In this episode Philip is drawn, by both an angel of the Lord and the Spirit of the Lord, even further toward the margins of the house of Israel. The fact that the next candidate for conversion and baptism is a eunuch has important prophetic resonances. For example, Isaiah 56:3-5, part of a vision of the restoration of Israel that Jesus quoted in his takeover of the temple (Luke 19:46), speaks of eunuchs finding a home and an imperishable name in the coming restoration. Since Luke will treat the later conversion of the centurion and his family as the breakthrough to the Gentiles, our author would have us understand the eunuch as a convert to Judaism. Yet his ethnicity as an Ethiopian is important to Luke's theme of the universality of the church's mission.

The text that the eunuch is reading aloud (v. 28) is Isaiah 53:7-8, from the famous fourth Servant Song, which Luke quotes only here in his two volumes. It is important to note that this is the Septuagint version, whose wording here differs significantly from the Hebrew. The wording of the

about someone else?" ³⁵Then Philip opened his mouth and, beginning with this scripture passage, he proclaimed Jesus to him. ³⁶As they traveled along the road they came to some water, and the eunuch said, "Look, there is water. What is to prevent my being baptized?"

[³⁷] ³⁸ Then he ordered the chariot to stop, and Philip and the eunuch both went down into the water, and he baptized him. ³⁹When they came out of the water, the Spirit of the Lord snatched Philip away, and the eunuch saw him no more, but continued on his way rejoicing. ⁴⁰Philip came to Azotus, and went about proclaiming the good news to all the towns until he reached Caesarea.

9 **Saul's Conversation.** ¹Now Saul, still breathing murderous threats against the disciples of the Lord, went to the high priest ²and asked him for letters to the synagogues in Damascus, that, if he should find any men or women who belonged to the Way, he might bring them back to Jerusalem in chains. ³On his journey, as he was nearing Damascus, a light from the sky

---

Old Greek is peculiarly open to being understood as applicable to the death and resurrection of Jesus. The rendering of Luke Timothy Johnson, in his *Acts of the Apostles* (Collegeville, Minn.: Liturgical Press, 1992), illustrates this well: "As a sheep led to the slaughter, and as silent as a lamb before its shearer, so he does not open his mouth. In his lowliness his judgment was taken away. Who will recite his generation? For his life is taken away from the earth." The application of this text to the childless Jesus would have a special appeal for the eunuch. Jesus' "generation" after he was "taken away" in resurrection is his growing band of post-Easter disciples, now including this eunuch.

Though he went to Jerusalem "to worship" (v. 27), as a eunuch he was explicitly prevented from entering beyond the Court of the Gentiles (see Deuteronomy 23:2, where eunuchs are banned from "the community of the Lord"). How different here, where his reception of the gospel of Jesus leads him to ask, "What is to prevent my being baptized?" Thus the one banned will indeed become a member of the community of the Lord.

Along with illustrating the spread of the word (1:8), this episode demonstrates the process of interpreting the Scriptures that Luke surely had in mind when he spoke of Jesus explaining to the disciples at Emmaus what referred to him in all the Scriptures "beginning with Moses and all the prophets" (Luke 24:27).

9:1-19 The conversion and commissioning of Saul

Although this key episode in the history of the church is traditionally called the "conversion" of Paul, it is not a conversion in the sense of

◄ suddenly flashed around him. ⁴He fell to the ground and heard a voice saying to him, "Saul, Saul, why are you persecuting me?" ⁵He said, "Who are you, sir?" The reply came, "I am Jesus, whom you are persecuting. ⁶Now get up and go into the city and you will be told what you must do." ⁷The men who were traveling with him stood speechless, for they heard the voice but could see no one. ⁸Saul got up from the ground, but when he opened his eyes he could see nothing; so they led him by the hand and brought him to Damascus. ⁹For three days he was unable to see, and he neither ate nor drank.

Saul's Baptism. ¹⁰There was a disciple in Damascus named Ananias, and the Lord said to him in a vision, "Ananias." He answered, "Here I am, Lord."

¹¹The Lord said to him, "Get up and go to the street called Straight and ask at the house of Judas for a man from Tarsus named Saul. He is there praying, ¹²and [in a vision] he has seen a man named Ananias come in and lay [his] hands on him, that he may regain his sight." ¹³But Ananias replied, "Lord, I ► have heard from many sources about this man, what evil things he has done to your holy ones in Jerusalem. ¹⁴And ► here he has authority from the chief priests to imprison all who call upon your name." ¹⁵But the Lord said to him, "Go, for this man is a chosen instrument of mine to carry my name before Gentiles, kings, and Israelites, ¹⁶and I will show him what he will have to suffer for my name." ¹⁷So Ananias went and entered the house; laying his

---

changing from one religion to another, for Saul/Paul does not cease to be a Jew; he moves from being a Jew who persecutes the growing "Jews for Jesus" group to being a Jew for Jesus himself.

Is this a conversion in another sense, namely, turning from an immoral life to a moral one? Even in his persecution of the church, Paul is zealously pursuing what he understands to be the will of God. Yet Luke describes Saul as "breathing murderous threats," which is at odds with the commandment against murder. And Luke's description of the martyrdom of Stephen (7:54–8:1) showed Saul minding the cloaks of those performing the "extra-legal" stoning and "consenting to this execution."

Further, the change from persecutor to promoter is surely some kind of transformation and reorientation. This has led some to call what happens to Paul a prophetic commissioning, for he is stopped in his tracks to be sent on a mission. Maybe it is best to say that this is both a conversion and a commissioning.

Luke describes the event as a theophany. It parallels the encounter of Moses with the divine Presence in Exodus 3. Like Moses, Saul is startled with a manifestation of brightness, hears his name called twice, hears the voice identify itself, and receives a commission.

hands on him, he said, "Saul, my brother, the Lord has sent me, Jesus who appeared to you on the way by which you came, that you may regain your sight and be filled with the holy Spirit." ¹⁸Immediately things like scales fell from his eyes and he regained his sight. He got up and was baptized, ¹⁹and when he had eaten, he recovered his strength.

Saul Preaches in Damascus. He stayed some days with the disciples in Damascus, ²⁰and he began at once to proclaim Jesus in the synagogues, that

he is the Son of God. ²¹All who heard him were astounded and said, "Is not this the man who in Jerusalem ravaged those who call upon this name, and came here expressly to take them back in chains to the chief priests?" ²²But Saul grew all the stronger and confounded [the] Jews who lived in Damascus, proving that this is the Messiah.

Saul Visits Jerusalem. ²³After a long time had passed, the Jews conspired to kill him, ²⁴but their plot became known to Saul. Now they were keeping watch on the gates day and night so as to kill

---

The revelation that he receives, "I am Jesus, whom you are persecuting," is a striking summation of a major theme of Paul's letters: the identification of the risen Lord with his church, which Paul elaborates in his treatment of the Christian community as the body of Christ, especially in Romans and 1 Corinthians.

When Paul addresses the voice in the vision as *Kyrie*, it most likely means "Lord" in the full sense of the appellation. The identification of that Lord as Jesus, then, parallels Stephen's calling Jesus "Lord" (7:59). That this title recurs twelve more times in this chapter suggests that Luke would have us understand this beginning of the mission to the Gentiles as a special manifestation of the lordship of the risen Jesus. For references to this experience in Paul's own words, see 1 Corinthians 9:1 ("Have I not seen Jesus our Lord?"); 2 Cor 4:4:6; Gal 1:12.

To this paradox of the enemy of the Christian movement becoming its greatest promoter, Luke adds another: when his eyes were opened, he could see nothing (v. 8). Though he became temporarily blind, he really did have, in a deeper sense, an "eye-opening" experience. The cure from that physical blindness that accompanies his baptism underscores his spiritual enlightenment. Luke will elaborate on this imagery in the later retellings of this episode in chapters 22 and 26.

Notice that our author has four different and suggestive ways of naming the growing church in this passage: "the disciples of the Lord" (v. 1); "the Way" (v. 2); "all who call upon your name" (v. 14, echoing Joel 2:32 quoted in Acts 2:21; and see Romans 10:13); and "the holy ones" (v. 13, a

him, ²⁵but his disciples took him one night and let him down through an opening in the wall, lowering him in a basket.

²⁶When he arrived in Jerusalem he tried to join the disciples, but they were all afraid of him, not believing that he was a disciple. ²⁷Then Barnabas took charge of him and brought him to the apostles, and he reported to them how on the way he had seen the Lord and that he had spoken to him, and how in Damascus he had spoken out boldly in the name of Jesus. ²⁸He moved about freely with them in Jerusalem, and spoke out boldly in the name of the Lord. ²⁹He also spoke and debated with the Hellenists, but they tried to kill him. ³⁰And when the brothers learned of this, they took him down to Caesarea and sent him on his way to Tarsus.

The Church at Peace. ³¹The church throughout all Judea, Galilee, and Samaria was at peace. It was being built up and walked in the fear of the Lord, and with the consolation of the holy Spirit it grew in numbers.

Peter Heals Aeneas at Lydda. ³²As Peter was passing through every region, he went down to the holy ones

---

Jewish term for Israel set apart for the Lord's service, here appropriated by Christian Jews, as Paul will do in his letters).

9:19b-31 Saul preaches in Damascus and visits Jerusalem

The adversary turned promoter begins his apostolic life right there in Damascus by preaching in the local synagogues that Jesus is the long-awaited Christ (Greek for the Hebrew term *Messiah*, or "Anointed One"). When Luke says that Saul proclaimed Jesus as the Son of God, he probably means this title in the same sense, that is, as Messiah (see Psalm 2:7). Later theology will apply it in the full sense of divinity, as in John 1:1, 18.

How Saul "will have to suffer" for the name of Jesus (v. 16) is soon demonstrated in the plot by the Jews of Damascus against his life (v. 23) and then in the similar efforts of the Jerusalem Hellenists (v. 29). In Jerusalem, it takes Barnabas's testimony to render him credible and acceptable to the local disciples. As in the case of Philip (8:14-17), the mission of the one whom later tradition will call "the Apostle" needs the seal of approval from the Jerusalem leadership. This Jerusalem sojourn is possibly the visit to which Paul refers, with a different emphasis, in Galatians 1:18-20.

In contrast to the cloak-and-dagger escapades that characterized Paul's debut as an apostle, the one-line summary at verse 31 describes the growth of the church throughout the entire area as peaceful and abundant.

9:32-43 Peter heals at Lydda and Joppa

Just how that growth mentioned in the summary of verse 31 occurred is illustrated by two episodes from Peter's healing ministry. Visiting a

living in Lydda. [33]There he found a man named Aeneas, who had been confined to bed for eight years, for he was paralyzed. [34]Peter said to him, "Aeneas, Jesus Christ heals you. Get up and make your bed." He got up at once. [35]And all the inhabitants of Lydda and Sharon saw him, and they turned to the Lord.

Peter Restores Tabitha to Life. [36]Now in Joppa there was a disciple named Tabitha (which translated means Dorcas). She was completely occupied with good deeds and almsgiving. [37]Now during those days she fell sick and died, so after washing her, they laid [her] out in a room upstairs. [38]Since Lydda was near Joppa, the disciples, hearing that Peter was there, sent two men to him with the request, "Please come to us without delay." [39]So Peter got up and went with them. When he arrived, they took him to the room upstairs where all the widows came to him weeping and showing him the tunics and cloaks that Dorcas had made while she was with them. [40]Peter sent them all out and knelt down and prayed. Then he turned to her body and said, "Tabitha, rise up." She opened her eyes, saw Peter, and sat up. [41]He gave her his hand and raised her up, and when he had called the holy ones and the widows, he presented her alive. [42]This became known all over Joppa, and many came to believe in the Lord. [43]And he stayed a long time in Joppa with Simon, a tanner.

Christian community ("the holy ones") in the plains town of Lydda, he heals a long-term paralytic named Aeneas. The sight of old Aeneas healed moves "all the inhabitants" to "turn to the Lord" (now shorthand for coming to Christian faith). Another exemplary disciple, Tabitha, falls sick and dies, apparently prematurely. Her resuscitation at Peter's command occasions the conversion of many in Joppa.

Commentators have noticed that the language Luke uses to describe these healings is reminiscent of the Deuteronomic historian's description of the wonder-working of Elijah and Elisha (1 Kgs 17:17-24; 2 Kgs 4:31-37). This further underscores Luke's presentation of the disciples as prophetic successors of Jesus, just as he is the prophet-like-Moses. They are not, however, successors in the sense of replacing Jesus; their ministry is an expression of the risen Lord Jesus working through them.

THE INAUGURATION OF THE GENTILE MISSION

Acts 10:1–15:35

Although Luke knows of others who brought the gospel to Gentiles (see the reference to Cypriot and Cyrenean Christians who evangelized Greeks in Antioch at 11:20), he chooses to focus on the experience of Peter,

IV. The Inauguration of the Gentile Mission

10 **The Vision of Cornelius.** ¹Now in Caesarea there was a man named Cornelius, a centurion of the Cohort called the Italica, ²devout and God-fearing along with his whole household, who used to give alms generously to the Jewish people and pray to God constantly. ³One afternoon about three o'clock, he saw plainly in a vision an angel of God come in to him and say to him, "Cornelius." ⁴He looked intently at him and, seized with fear, said, "What is it, sir?" He said to him, "Your prayers and almsgiving have ascended as a memorial offering before God. ⁵Now send some men to Joppa and summon one Simon who is called Peter. ⁶He is staying with another Simon, a tanner, who has a house by the sea." ⁷When the angel who spoke to him had left, he called two of

who was divinely led in this direction in dramatic ways. The accounts of Herod Agrippa's persecution of Christians, followed by his own punitive death, then the first mission of Paul (Acts 13–14), all lead naturally to the Council of Jerusalem (Acts 15), which resolves an important policy question raised by this unexpected success among the nations.

10:1-33 Visions and revisions: the mission of Peter to Cornelius

To describe the change that Peter undergoes in chapter 10 as a "conversion" might seem strange to our way of thinking, but Luke clearly sees this transformation of Peter as parallel to Paul's "conversion" in importance. Paul changed from seeing the Jesus movement as a threat to the will of God to seeing it as the very fulfillment of God's plan. Similarly, Peter is moved from perceiving the messianic movement as a Jews-only affair to understanding it as God's blessing for Gentiles as well. Although this vision is implied in Peter's second speech (see 3:25), it takes the divine interventions portrayed in the present chapter to enable Peter to see the practical consequences of the promise to Abraham that his descendants would be a blessing for "all the nations of the earth" (Gen 18:18; 22:18). Thus, as in the case of Paul's transformation, Luke will tell the story of Peter's change three times. In both transformations, the initiative is not human but divine.

Cornelius is a "God fear[er]." This is not a formal social classification but a description of a Gentile who, without formally joining the people of Israel (entailing circumcision for males), has taken on Jewish beliefs and pious practices such as almsgiving and prayer at the hour of temple worship.

Luke underscores the fact that the actions of both Cornelius and Peter are divinely prompted by linking their actions to interlocking visions. The angel of God makes it clear to Cornelius that the intervention is a response to his prayer and tells him to send for Peter at Simon the tanner's place.

51

his servants and a devout soldier from his staff, [8]explained everything to them, and sent them to Joppa.

The Vision of Peter. [9]The next day, while they were on their way and nearing the city, Peter went up to the roof terrace to pray at about noontime. [10]He was hungry and wished to eat, and while they were making preparations he fell into a trance. [11]He saw heaven opened and something resembling a large sheet coming down, lowered to the ground by its four corners. [12]In it were all the earth's four-legged animals and reptiles and the birds of the sky. [13]A voice said to him, "Get up, Peter. Slaughter and eat." [14]But Peter said, "Certainly not, sir. For never have I eaten anything profane and unclean." [15]The voice spoke to him again, a second time, "What God has made clean,

you are not to call profane." [16]This happened three times, and then the object was taken up into the sky.

[17]While Peter was in doubt about the meaning of the vision he had seen, the men sent by Cornelius asked for Simon's house and arrived at the entrance. [18]They called out inquiring whether Simon, who is called Peter, was staying there. [19]As Peter was pondering the vision, the Spirit said [to him], "There are three men here looking for you. [20]So get up, go downstairs, and accompany them without hesitation, because I have sent them." [21]Then Peter went down to the men and said, "I am the one you are looking for. What is the reason for your being here?" [22]They answered, "Cornelius, a centurion, an upright and God-fearing man, respected by the whole Jewish nation,

---

Peter's vision confronts him (three times!) with a powerful puzzlement: shown a sheet full of clean and unclean animals, he is instructed to kill and eat. In effect, this is a command to ignore a primary Jewish identity marker. (It also evokes the cosmic covenant God made with Noah in Genesis 9, where Noah and family, representing all humanity, were given "every creature that is alive" to eat, Gen 9:3.)

When the messengers from Cornelius, presumably Gentiles, arrive at Simon's place with the account of their master's visions, Peter's readiness to offer them hospitality indicates that he has begun to learn the lesson of the animal vision: if all animals are clean, the major social barrier between Gentile and Jew has been eliminated. Peter himself states at verse 28 that he has learned this lesson.

Several elements suggest that, though he is only a "God-fear[er]" (a Gentile worshiper of YHWH, but not a full-fledged convert), Cornelius's piety has achieved a kind of temple intimacy with God. The angelic vision happens "about three o'clock" (vv. 3 and 30; literally "the ninth hour," the time of the afternoon sacrifice, in the spirit of Psalm 141:2, Judith 9:1, and Daniel 9:21). His prayers and almsgiving have reached God "as a memor-

was directed by a holy angel to summon you to his house and to hear what you have to say." [23]So he invited them in and showed them hospitality.

The next day he got up and went with them, and some of the brothers from Joppa went with him. [24]On the following day he entered Caesarea. Cornelius was expecting them and had called together his relatives and close friends. [25]When Peter entered, Cornelius met him and, falling at his feet, paid him homage. [26]Peter, however, raised him up, saying, "Get up. I myself am also a human being." [27]While he conversed with him, he went in and found many people gathered together [28]and said to them, "You know that it is unlawful for a Jewish man to associate with, or visit, a Gentile, but God has shown me that I should not call any person profane or unclean. [29]And that is why I came without objection when sent for. May I ask, then, why you summoned me?"

[30]Cornelius replied, "Four days ago at this hour, three o'clock in the afternoon, I was at prayer in my house when suddenly a man in dazzling robes stood before me and said, [31]'Cornelius, your prayer has been heard and your almsgiving remembered before God. [32]Send therefore to Joppa and summon Simon, who is called Peter. He is a guest in the house of Simon, a tanner, by the sea.' [33]So I sent for you immediately, and you were kind enough to come. Now therefore we are all here in the presence of God to listen to all that you have been commanded by the Lord."

Peter's Speech. [34]Then Peter proceeded to speak and said, "In truth, I see that God shows no partiality. [35]Rather, in ▶

---

ial offering before God" (v. 4; and see v. 31), and he can refer to his own "non-kosher" home as "here in the presence of God" (v. 33, a phrase whose Old Testament connotation is the temple presence of God, as in Leviticus 4:4, 18, 24). Sacred space now extends to wherever people respond to the will of God.

10:34-48 Peter evangelizes Cornelius and his household

Peter's speech to the household of Cornelius is a rich résumé of Lukan theology. God shows no partiality, but whoever fears him and acts uprightly is acceptable to God (*dektos*, "acceptable," or "accepted," like a valid temple sacrifice). This principle does not address the contemporary question of religious pluralism but rather the first-century question of who is a candidate for God's messianic blessing. The reference is to persons like Cornelius and company: no matter what their ethnic identity, as long as they are receptive to God's revelation through the people Israel and do what is right, they are acceptable to God.

Peter can speak of the whole life of Jesus as God proclaiming "peace through Jesus Christ" (v. 36, alluding to Isa 52:7). When he refers to "how God *anointed* Jesus of Nazareth with . . . Spirit and power" (v. 38, emphasis

every nation whoever fears him and acts uprightly is acceptable to him. [36]You know the word [that] he sent to the Israelites as he proclaimed peace through Jesus Christ, who is Lord of all, [37]what has happened all over Judea, beginning in Galilee after the baptism that John preached, [38]how God anointed Jesus of Nazareth with the holy Spirit and power. He went about doing good and healing all those oppressed by the devil, for God was with him. [39]We are witnesses of all that he did both in the country of the Jews and [in] Jerusalem. They put him to death by hanging him on a tree. [40]This man God raised [on] the third day and granted that he be visible, [41]not to all the people, but to us, the witnesses chosen by God in advance, who ate and drank with him after he rose from the dead. [42]He commissioned us to preach to the people and testify that he is the one appointed by God as judge of the living and the dead. [43]To him all the prophets bear witness, that everyone who believes in him will receive forgiveness of sins through his name."

The Baptism of Cornelius. [44]While Peter was still speaking these things, the holy Spirit fell upon all who were listening to the word. [45]The circumcised believers who had accompanied Peter were astounded that the gift of the holy Spirit should have been poured out on the Gentiles also, [46]for they could hear them speaking in tongues and glorify-

added), he is rooting Jesus' title of "Christ" in the prophetic anointing for mission interpreted by Isaiah 61:1 at Luke 4:18. Fittingly for this context, he calls Jesus "Lord of *all*" and "the one appointed by God as judge of the living and the dead" (emphasis added).

The action of the Spirit is said to interrupt Peter's speech, but in fact Luke has communicated fully to his readers. The *shalom* ("peace") that God has proclaimed to Israel through Jesus is meant for all. And God presently demonstrates that thesis by way of the endowment of the Holy Spirit upon Cornelius's receptive household. Pointedly, Luke notes that "the circumcised believers who had accompanied Peter were astounded that the *gift of the holy Spirit* should have been *poured out* on the Gentiles also, for they could hear them *speaking in tongues* and glorifying God" (v. 45, emphasis added). The language is carefully chosen to recall the Pentecostal outpouring of the holy Spirit in chapter 2 (see 2:17, 18, 33, 38). That the gift of the Spirit should precede baptism in the name of Jesus demonstrates, again, that the mission to the Gentiles is God's will. It also shows that circumcision is not required for entry into the messianic people of God.

Christian tradition will honor another person, Paul, as the Apostle to the Gentiles par excellence (indeed, Paul identifies himself that way in Galatians 2:7), but Luke has made it clear that that mission was authenticated by no less a person than the chief of the apostles, Peter. And Peter was simply responding to the initiative of God.

ing God. Then Peter responded, [47]"Can anyone withhold the water for baptizing these people, who have received the holy Spirit even as we have?" [48]He ordered them to be baptized in the name of Jesus Christ. [49]Then they invited him to stay for a few days.

11 **The Baptism of the Gentiles Explained.** [1]Now the apostles and the brothers who were in Judea heard that the Gentiles too had accepted the word of God. [2]So when Peter went up to Jerusalem the circumcised believers confronted him, [3]saying, "You entered the house of uncircumcised people and ate with them." [4]Peter began and explained it to them step by step, saying,

[5]"I was at prayer in the city of Joppa when in a trance I had a vision, something resembling a large sheet coming down, lowered from the sky by its four corners, and it came to me. [6]Looking intently into it, I observed and saw the four-legged animals of the earth, the wild beasts, the reptiles, and the birds of the sky. [7]I also heard a voice say to me, 'Get up, Peter. Slaughter and eat.' [8]But I said, 'Certainly not, sir, because nothing profane or unclean has ever entered my mouth.' [9]But a second time a voice from heaven answered, 'What God has made clean, you are not to call profane.' [10]This happened three times, and then everything was drawn up again into the sky.

In the broader framework of the narrative in Acts, Peter's journey from Jewish Joppa to Roman Caesarea (10:23-24) is a miniature of the word journey from Jerusalem to Rome.

11:1-18 Peter explains God's actions to the Jerusalem authorities

As Simon Peter needed three similar visions to begin to fathom God's intentions regarding Jewish-Christian relations to the Gentiles, so Luke himself deems it necessary that this turn to the Gentiles be told three times. As in the case of Saul's conversion/call, our author first narrates the events directly (Acts 10) and then provides two interpretations of those events in subsequent speeches (chs. 11 and 15).

Since Peter's acceptance of Gentile hospitality is a violation of Jewish law, and his extension of the messianic renewal to the Gentiles was done without authorization from the Jerusalem church authorities, the apostles rightly demand an explanation. The recital of Peter's rooftop visions of the menagerie in the linen sheet, the embassy from Cornelius's house, the visit, the account of Cornelius's vision—all this is familiar enough to us who have read chapter 11. But what follows presents five fresh elements of interpretation.

First, the experience of Cornelius's household in their response in faith to the preaching of Peter is described as being "saved" (v. 14; compare with Acts 2:47). Second, Peter equates their experience of the holy Spirit

11Just then three men appeared at the house where we were, who had been sent to me from Caesarea. 12The Spirit told me to accompany them without discriminating. These six brothers also went with me, and we entered the man's house. 13He related to us how he had seen [the] angel standing in his house, saying, 'Send someone to Joppa and summon Simon, who is called Peter, 14who will speak words to you by which you and all your household will be saved.' 15As I began to speak, the holy Spirit fell upon them as it had upon us at the beginning, 16and I remembered the word of the Lord, how he had said, 'John baptized with water but you will be baptized with the holy Spirit.' 17If then God gave them the same gift he gave to us when we came to believe in the Lord Jesus Christ, who was I to be able to hinder God?" 18When they heard this, they stopped objecting and glorified God, saying, "God has then granted life-giving repentance to the Gentiles too."

The Church at Antioch. 19Now those who had been scattered by the persecution that arose because of Stephen went as far as Phoenicia, Cyprus, and Antioch, preaching the word to no one but Jews. 20There were

with the apostles' own experience on Pentecost, pointedly referred to as "the beginning" (v. 15). Third, these endowments of the Spirit are, for the first time, described as what John the Baptist and Jesus meant by being "baptized with the holy Spirit" (v. 16; see Luke 3:16 for John's word and Acts 1:5 for Jesus'). Fourth, Peter refers to the Pentecost experience as the moment when he and the rest of the Twelve "came to believe in the Lord Jesus Christ" (v. 17); this implies that their initial discipleship during Jesus' earthly ministry had not yet constituted full Christian faith. Full Christian faith requires acceptance of Jesus as risen Lord and the gift of the holy Spirit. Finally, the Jerusalem leaders view the Cornelius episode not simply as a singular episode but as a paradigm of what God wills: "God has then granted life-giving repentance to the Gentiles too" (v. 18).

11:19-30 The Antioch mission

Although Luke has highlighted Peter's encounter with Cornelius as the paradigmatic and authoritative breakthrough, this passage makes it clear that the word has been reaching the Gentiles through other agents as well. In the wake of the persecution that followed the martyrdom of Stephen, Jerusalem messianists (Christians) brought the word to Greek-speaking Jews from Cyprus and Cyrene, and these in turn evangelized Greeks (Gentiles) up in Antioch of Syria.

As in the case of Peter and Cornelius, this outreach to Gentiles in Antioch is ratified by Jerusalem authorization: the elders send Barnabas, who in turn enlists the help of Saul of Tarsus. When Luke says Barnabas "en-

some Cypriots and Cyrenians among them, however, who came to Antioch and began to speak to the Greeks as well, proclaiming the Lord Jesus. [21]The hand of the Lord was with them and a great number who believed turned to the Lord. [22]The news about them reached the ears of the church in Jerusalem, and they sent Barnabas [to go] to Antioch. [23]When he arrived and saw the grace of God, he rejoiced and encouraged them all to remain faithful to the Lord in firmness of heart, [24]for he was a good man, filled with the holy Spirit and faith. And a large number of people was added to the Lord. [25]Then he went to Tarsus to look for Saul, [26]and when he had found him he brought him to Anti-och. For a whole year they met with the church and taught a large number of people, and it was in Antioch that the disciples were first called Christians.

The Prediction of Agabus. [27]At that time some prophets came down from Jerusalem to Antioch, [28]and one of them named Agabus stood up and predicted by the Spirit that there would be a severe famine all over the world, and it happened under Claudius. [29]So the disciples determined that, according to ability, each should send relief to the brothers who lived in Judea. [30]This they did, sending it to the presbyters in care of Barnabas and Saul.

12 Herod's Persecution of the Christians. [1]About that time King

---

couraged" the people to remain faithful (v. 23), he may be hinting at the meaning of his nickname (Barnabas = "son of consolation"), which he said the apostles applied to this Levite from Cyprus (see 4:36).

In Paul's letter to the Galatians, he refers to himself as "entrusted with the gospel to the uncircumcised, just as Peter to the circumcised" (Gal 2:7). If this seems to be at odds with Luke's portrayal of Peter's evangelization of the household of Cornelius, it should be noted that Paul nowhere claims to be the *first* missioner to the Gentiles. And Luke does give us significant episodes about Peter's evangelizing the circumcised (Acts 2–5; 9:32-43). Nor do we hear of Peter spending much more time among the uncircumcised.

Having described the developments of a mixed (Jewish-Gentile) church in Antioch, which is emerging as an entity distinct enough to warrant a special name, *hoi Christianoi* ("Christians," the first use of the name), Luke illustrates their solidarity with the Jewish-Christian brothers and sisters in Judea. Responding to Agabus's prophecy about imminent widespread famine, the Antiochenes send relief to the Jerusalem elders.

12:1-25 Great reversals: Peter's escape and Herod's death

This book called the Acts of the Apostles turns out to be mainly about the acts of *two* apostles, Peter and Paul. Up to this point, Peter has dominated

Herod laid hands upon some members of the church to harm them. [2]He had James, the brother of John, killed by the sword, [3]and when he saw that this was pleasing to the Jews he proceeded to arrest Peter also. (It was [the] feast of Unleavened Bread.) [4]He had him taken into custody and put in prison under the guard of four squads of four soldiers each. He intended to bring him before the people after Passover. [5]Peter thus was being kept in prison, but prayer by the church was fervently being made to God on his behalf.

[6]On the very night before Herod was to bring him to trial, Peter, secured by double chains, was sleeping between two soldiers, while outside the door guards kept watch on the prison. [7]Suddenly the angel of the Lord stood by him and a light shone in the cell. He tapped Peter on the side and awakened him, saying, "Get up quickly." The chains fell from his wrists. [8]The angel said to him, "Put on your belt and your sandals." He did so. Then he said to him, "Put on your cloak and follow me." [9]So he followed him out, not realizing that what was happening through the angel was real; he thought he was seeing a vision. [10]They passed the first guard, then the second, and came to the iron gate leading out to the city, which opened for them by itself. They emerged

---

the stage. In the present chapter, Luke rounds off the story of Peter before taking up in earnest the missions of Paul.

Using as his centerpiece a favorite genre of Hellenistic entertainment, the "great escape" story, Luke vividly illustrates divine power at work through accounts of vivid reversals and transitions.

First there is the transition from James to James. The third of four Herods mentioned in Luke-Acts, Herod Agrippa I, the grandson of Herod the Great, has James of Zebedee, one of the Twelve, killed by the sword. No motive is given. Before the chapter closes (v. 17), it is clear that the key Jerusalem leader is not one of the Twelve but another James, the brother of the Lord. To underscore the fact that the followers of Jesus relive his story (recall especially the martyrdom of Stephen in chapters 6 and 7), Luke notes that this persecution by Herod occurs during Passover time.

Divine power and justice are displayed in the dramatic reversal experienced by Herod. The chapter begins with the king's arrogant and violent exercise of power in arbitrary persecution, execution, and arrest; it ends with Herod's being hailed as a god, only to suffer an ignominious death. Notice that this idolatry occurs in the secular capital, Caesarea (Maritima), and the idolaters are a pagan embassy from Tyre and Sidon. This is one of a series of examples in Acts showing how Gentiles can be idolatrous in their theism. And Tyre was famous for its propensity to treat a man as a god (see Ezek 28).

and made their way down an alley, and suddenly the angel left him. ¹¹Then Peter recovered his senses and said, "Now I know for certain that [the] Lord sent his angel and rescued me from the hand of Herod and from all that the Jewish people had been expecting." ¹²When he realized this, he went to the house of Mary, the mother of John who is called Mark, where there were many people gathered in prayer. ¹³When he knocked on the gateway door, a maid named Rhoda came to answer it. ¹⁴She was so overjoyed when she recognized Peter's voice that, instead of opening the gate, she ran in and announced that Peter was standing at the gate. ¹⁵They told her, "You are out of your mind," but she insisted that it was so. But they kept saying, "It is his angel." ¹⁶But Peter continued to knock, and when they opened it, they saw him and were astounded. ¹⁷He motioned to them with his hand to be quiet and explained [to them] how the Lord had led him out of the prison, and said, "Report this to James and the brothers." Then he left and went to another place. ¹⁸At daybreak there was no small commotion among the soldiers over what had become of Peter. ¹⁹Herod, after instituting a search but not finding him, ordered the guards tried and executed. Then he left Judea to spend some time in Caesarea.

Herod's Death. ²⁰He had long been very angry with the people of Tyre and Sidon, who now came to him in a body. After winning over Blastus, the king's

---

Another subtle transition that Luke signals here is the growing division between the minority group called "the church" (vv. 1 and 5) and the Jewish majority. At the end of his Gospel and the beginning of Acts, Luke was careful to stress that the first Christians were, and remained, practicing Jews. Then, describing the plot of the Jewish community in Damascus against Paul, Luke could state simply, "the Jews conspired to kill him" (9:23). Now here in chapter 12 Luke can refer to Agrippa's persecution of the church as "pleasing to the Jews" (v. 3), and Peter can speak of his rescue "from the hand of Herod and from all that the Jewish people had been expecting" (v. 11). While Jews will continue to join the growing church, the hostility between this minority and the majority begins to deepen.

These transitions and reversals frame the marvelous escape of Peter. Luke's interest in paralleling God's work in the mission of Jesus and the church with the divine liberating action of the Exodus continues here. As in Exodus (3:2; 4:24 LXX; 14:19; 23:20, 23; 32:34), an angel of the Lord is instrumental in leading the action (vv. 7-11, 15, 23). The biblical word for smiting (*patassō*) is used playfully here to point up the contrast between the gentle smiting that the angel uses to awaken Peter (v. 7) and the fatal smiting of Herod at the end (v. 23), reminiscent of the smiting of Sennacherib's troops by the angel of the Lord in 2 Kings 19. As in the story of

chamberlain, they sued for peace because their country was supplied with food from the king's territory. [21]On an appointed day, Herod, attired in royal robes, [and] seated on the rostrum, addressed them publicly. [22]The assembled crowd cried out, "This is the voice of a god, not of a man." [23]At once the angel of the Lord struck him down because he did not ascribe the honor to God, and he was eaten by worms and breathed his last. [24]But the word of God continued to spread and grow.

Mission of Barnabas and Saul. [25]After Barnabas and Saul completed their relief mission, they returned to Jerusalem, taking with them John, who is called Mark.

13 [1]Now there were in the church at Antioch prophets and teachers: Barnabas, Symeon who was called Niger, Lucius of Cyrene, Manaen who was a close friend of Herod the tetrarch, and Saul. [2]While they were worshiping the Lord and fasting, the holy Spirit said, "Set apart for me Barnabas and Saul for the work to which I have called them." [3]Then, completing their fasting and prayer, they laid hands on them and sent them off.

God's dealings with Israel in the Hebrew Bible (Old Testament), the same divine power continues to bring both liberation and reprisal. Luke's dwelling with such zest on these events fits well the spirit of a book whose final word, describing Paul's unstoppable preaching while under house arrest, is *akōlytōs* ("unhindered").

The return of Barnabas and Saul to Antioch after completing their "relief mission" (*diakonia*) to the poor of Jerusalem (v. 25) completes the excursion begun at 11:30. This is likely the visit to which Paul refers in Galatians 2:1-10, when "the pillars" (James, Cephas, and John) urged Paul to continue being "mindful of the poor."

Acts 13:1-3 From five leaders, two missioners: the sending of Barnabas and Saul

Having rounded off the story of Peter's leadership of the early church, Luke now picks up the story of Paul, which will dominate the remainder of the book. Indeed, this second half of the history could well be called "The Acts of Paul." An illustrious quintet of church prophets and teachers—including one Simeon called *the black* (Niger), an African (Lucius from Cyrene), and a childhood companion of Herod Antipas—are pictured here fasting and praying. Barnabas and Saul are chosen by the holy Spirit (in prophecy, presumably) and sent off to do what the Spirit calls "the work." The work, of course, is what the quotation from Habakkuk at verse 41 calls what God is doing and something that the scoffers will never believe.

First Mission Begins in Cyprus. [4]So they, sent forth by the holy Spirit, went down to Seleucia and from there sailed to Cyprus. [5]When they arrived in Salamis, they proclaimed the word of God in the Jewish synagogues. They had John also as their assistant. [6]When they had traveled through the whole island as far as Paphos, they met a magician named Bar-Jesus who was a Jewish false prophet. [7]He was with the proconsul Sergius Paulus, a man of intelligence, who had summoned Barnabas and Saul and wanted to hear the word of God. [8]But Elymas the magician (for that is what his name means) opposed them in an attempt to turn the proconsul away from the faith. [9]But Saul, also known as Paul, filled with the holy Spirit, looked intently at him [10]and said, "You son of the devil, you enemy of all that is right, full of every sort of deceit and fraud. Will you not stop twisting the straight paths of [the] Lord? [11]Even now the hand of the Lord is upon you. You will be blind, and unable to see the sun for a time." Immediately a dark mist fell upon him, and he went about seeking people to lead him by the hand. [12]When the proconsul saw what had happened, he came to believe, for he was astonished by the teaching about the Lord.

Paul's Arrival at Antioch in Pisidia. [13]From Paphos, Paul and his companions set sail and arrived at Perga in

13:4-13 Barnabas, Saul, and John Mark evangelize Cyprus

This first outreach of the person that Christian tradition will call "the Apostle to the Gentiles" is a reprise of elements that characterized the first outreach of Philip to the Samaritans and then that of Peter to the Gentile household of Cornelius. As Philip met, in the person of Simon Magus, the power of evil present in the pagan world of magic and overcame that power with the Spirit of God, here the three Antiochene missioners encounter that same dark power in the person of a magician who happens to be an apostate Jew, Elymas bar-Jesus. Note that the Apostle, first introduced with his Jewish name, Saul, at the stoning of Stephen (Acts 7:58), is now called by his Latin name, Paul (v. 9; possibly a nickname, since *paulus* means "little"), probably because his mission will mainly address Gentiles from now on.

Paul taunts the magician, accusing him of reversing the plan of God, "twisting the straight paths of [the] Lord" (compare Luke 3:5, quoting Isaiah 40:3-5, "winding roads shall be made straight"). And Elymas's punishment of blindness parallels Paul's temporary fate when he was stopped in his tracks bent on resisting the plan of God in the community of the Way in Damascus (see Acts 9:6-11, where Paul, temporarily blinded, is sent to Straight Street!). Luke says that they evangelize the island from stem to stern (from Salamis in the east to Paphos in the west), but he

Pamphylia. But John left them and returned to Jerusalem. [14]They continued on from Perga and reached Antioch in Pisidia. On the sabbath they entered [into] the synagogue and took their seats. [15]After the reading of the law and the prophets, the synagogue officials sent word to them, "My brothers, if one of you has a word of exhortation for the people, please speak."

Paul's address in the Synagogue. [16]So Paul got up, motioned with his hand, and said, "Fellow Israelites and you others who are God-fearing, listen. [17]The God of this people Israel chose our ancestors and exalted the people during their sojourn in the land of Egypt. With uplifted arm he led them out of it [18]and for about forty years he put up with them in the desert. [19]When he had destroyed seven nations in the land of Canaan, he gave them their land as an inheritance [20]at the end of about four hundred and fifty years. After these things he provided judges up to Samuel [the] prophet. [21]Then they asked for a king. God gave them Saul, son of Kish, a man from the tribe of Benjamin, for forty years. [22]Then he removed him and raised up David as their king; of him he testified, 'I have found David, son of Jesse, a man after my own heart; he will carry out my every wish.' [23]From this man's descendants God, according to his promise, has brought to Israel a savior, Jesus. [24]John heralded his coming by proclaiming a baptism of repentance to all the people of Israel; [25]and as John was completing his course, he would say,

details only the conversion of the island's governor, Sergius Paulus, Paul's first Gentile disciple. Sergius is for Paul what Cornelius was for Peter.

13:14-52 Paul preaches in a synagogue in Pisidian Antioch

Although the name Galatia does not appear during this first missionary journey, Paul and Barnabas's ministry in Antioch of Pisidia (to be distinguished from Antioch of Syria, some three hundred miles to the east), and then in Iconium, Lystra, and Derbe, takes them into the southern part of that Roman province. Since we have no evidence that Paul evangelized farther north in Galatia, these are likely the "churches of Galatia" that Paul addressed in his famous letter by that name (Gal 1:2 and see 1 Cor 16:1).

As Peter began his post-Easter apostolic career with a speech proclaiming the life, death, and resurrection of Jesus in the light of the Hebrew Scriptures (Acts 2), Paul now does the same. Like Peter, Paul first addresses his message to his fellow Jews and to Gentile "God fear[ers]." As in the case of Peter's Pentecost speech, we can detect the hand of historian Luke employing the *pesher* technique, that is, using ancient texts to interpret recent events in the life of the community in the light of Easter faith.

'What do you suppose that I am? I am not he. Behold, one is coming after me; I am not worthy to unfasten the sandals of his feet.' ²⁶"My brothers, children of the family of Abraham, and those others among you who are God-fearing, to us this word of salvation has been sent. ²⁷The inhabitants of Jerusalem and their leaders failed to recognize him, and by condemning him they fulfilled the oracles of the prophets that are read sabbath after sabbath. ²⁸For even though they found no grounds for a death sentence, they asked Pilate to have him put to death, ²⁹and when they had accomplished all that was written about him, they took him down from the tree and placed him in a tomb. ³⁰But God raised him from the dead, ³¹and for many days he appeared to those who had come up with him from Galilee to Jerusalem. These are [now] his witnesses before the people. ³²We ourselves are proclaiming this good news to you that what God promised our ancestors ³³he has brought to fulfillment for us, [their] children, by raising up Jesus, as it is written in the second psalm, 'You are my son; this day I have begotten you.' ³⁴And that he raised him from the dead never to return to corruption he declared in this way, 'I shall give you the benefits assured to David.' ³⁵That is

---

The scene is reminiscent of Jesus' speech in the synagogue at Nazareth (Luke 4:14-30). The local Jewish community is gathered for readings from Scripture followed by interpretive preaching. In broad strokes Paul rehearses the familiar highlights of God's special relationship with Israel: the exodus from Egypt, the desert period, the conquest, and the kingship (Saul and David). Then he "fast forwards" to the coming of Jesus as savior of Israel, heralded by John. The phrase "according to his promise" (v. 23), in this context referring to Jesus as descendant of David, seems to have Nathan's prophecy to David especially in view (2 Sam 7:12-14) .

The second half of the speech, concerning the death and resurrection of Jesus and the mission of the church, draws even more heavily on biblical references to interpret the Christian experience.

As we have come to expect from Luke, blame for the death of Jesus is assigned to both Jewish and Roman leaders. Yet the death is interpreted as the fulfillment of "the oracles of the prophets" and "all that was written about him" (vv. 27, 29). Earlier parts of Luke-Acts have taught us some of the Scripture passages to which such statements refer—for example, Isaiah 53:7-8 (Acts 8:32-33); Psalm 31:6 (Luke 23:46); and the stories of Joseph and Moses in the Torah exemplifying the pattern of the rejected leader who becomes a savior (Acts 7:9-38).

When it comes to the resurrection, the Old Testament references become more abundant and explicit. Reference to "raising up" the son of

why he also says in another psalm, 'You will not suffer your holy one to see corruption.' ³⁶Now David, after he had served the will of God in his lifetime, fell asleep, was gathered to his ancestors, and did see corruption. ³⁷But the one whom God raised up did not see corruption. ³⁸You must know, my brothers, that through him forgiveness of sins is being proclaimed to you, [and] in regard to everything from which you could not be justified under the law of Moses, ³⁹in him every believer is justified. ⁴⁰Be careful, then, that what was said in the prophets not come about:

⁴¹'Look on, you scoffers,
be amazed and disappear.
For I am doing a work in your days,
a work that you will never believe even if someone tells you.' "

⁴²As they were leaving, they invited them to speak on these subjects the following sabbath. ⁴³After the congregation had dispersed, many Jews and worshipers who were converts to Judaism followed Paul and Barnabas, who spoke to them and urged them to remain faithful to the grace of God.

David (v. 33), also to be known as Son of God, gives new meaning to 2 Samuel 7:12-14 ("I will raise up your heir after you. . . . I will be a father to him, and he shall be a son to me"). The quotation of Psalm 2:7 in verse 33 ("You are my son; this day I have begotten you") interprets the resurrection as a moment of accession to the throne as king of Israel. Thus the same verse that we first heard at the scene by the Jordan ("You are my beloved Son," Luke 3:22), referring there to divine sonship and introducing a genealogy extending back to "Adam, son of God," here takes on a further dimension—the messianic one.

The quotation of Isaiah 55:3 ("I shall give you the benefits assured to David") becomes even more meaningful when we discover that the immediate context of that verse in Isaiah includes reference to an everlasting covenant (v. 2) and a mission to the Gentiles (v. 4). As in Luke 24:46-47, all three realities—the death and resurrection of the Messiah and the mission of the church—are grounded in Scripture. The use of Psalm 16:7 ("You will not suffer your holy one to see corruption"), fulfilled not in David but in the resurrection of Jesus, echoes the interpretation that Peter made at the heart of his Pentecost speech (Acts 2:25-31).

The language about justification through faith in verses 38-39 shows Paul using language that is characteristic of his letters, especially Romans and Galatians.

Although this speech gets a positive response and "many" in that synagogue congregation follow Paul and Barnabas, when "almost the whole city" (v. 44) turns out, no doubt including a majority of Gentiles, the (un-

Address to the Gentiles. ⁴⁴On the following sabbath almost the whole city gathered to hear the word of the Lord. ⁴⁵When the Jews saw the crowds, they were filled with jealousy and with violent abuse contradicted what Paul said. ⁴⁶Both Paul and Barnabas spoke out boldly and said, "It was necessary that the word of God be spoken to you first, but since you reject it and condemn yourselves as unworthy of eternal life, we now turn to the Gentiles. ⁴⁷For so the Lord has commanded us, 'I have made you a light to the Gentiles, that you may be an instrument of salvation to the ends of the earth.' "

⁴⁸The Gentiles were delighted when they heard this and glorified the word of the Lord. All who were destined for eternal life came to believe, ⁴⁹and the word of the Lord continued to spread through the whole region. ⁵⁰The Jews, however, incited the women of prominence who were worshipers and the leading men of the city, stirred up a persecution against Paul and Barnabas, and expelled them from their territory. ⁵¹So they shook the dust from their feet

---

persuaded) Jews begin to contradict Paul. This prompts a final invocation of Scripture, announcing both continuity and novelty. The passage from Isaiah that Simeon alluded to in his canticle at the presentation of Jesus in the temple (Luke 2:29-32) Paul quotes in full (v. 47): "I have made you a light to the Gentiles, that you may be an instrument of salvation to the ends of the earth" (Isa 49:6b). What Simeon applied to Jesus, Paul now applies to himself and Barnabas as exponents of the Christian mission. Indeed, Paul had just declared, ". . . through him [Jesus] forgiveness of sins is being proclaimed to you" (v. 38). That is, the risen Lord Jesus is now working through the likes of Paul and Barnabas. The novelty is that Jewish rejection of the good news triggers a turn to the Gentiles (v. 46).

With painful irony Luke shows that what was originally understood as the Jewish mission to be a "light to the Gentiles" now leaves many Jews behind. That Paul and Barnabas can later return to Pisidian Antioch to strengthen the disciples there and appoint elders (14:21-23) indicates that they left behind a community of believers (presumably composed of the Jews and converted Gentiles mentioned in 13:43) when they first left this town.

Does the strong language of Paul in verses 46-47 mean that God has abandoned the chosen people because of their unbelief? That interpretation has been the first step of Christian anti-Semitism. Luke's point is rather that which is reflected in Paul's own letters: the gospel is meant for Jews first, then Gentiles (see Rom 1:16; 9:24; 10:12). Another purpose is to present a paradigm of early Christian mission experience: the message will be accepted by some Jews and Gentiles and rejected by others, but

in protest against them and went to Iconium. [52]The disciples were filled with joy and the holy Spirit.

14 Paul and Barnabas at Iconium.
[1]In Iconium they entered the Jewish synagogue together and spoke in such a way that a great number of both Jews and Greeks came to believe, [2]although the disbelieving Jews stirred up and poisoned the minds of the Gentiles against the brothers. [3]So they stayed for a considerable period, speaking out boldly for the Lord, who confirmed the word about his grace by granting signs and wonders to occur through their hands. [4]The people of the city were divided: some were with the Jews; others, with the apostles. [5]When there was an attempt by both the Gentiles and the Jews, together with their leaders, to attack and stone them, [6]they realized it and fled to the Lycaonian cities of Lystra and Derbe and to the surrounding countryside, [7]where they continued to proclaim the good news.

Paul and Barnabas at Lystra. [8]At Lystra there was a crippled man, lame from birth, who had never walked. [9]He listened to Paul speaking, who looked intently at him, saw that he had the

---

God will use this rejection as an occasion for the advance of the mission (which is also Paul's interpretation in Romans 11). Paul will continue to address Jews first as his mode of operating, for example, in Iconium (14:1), Thessalonica (17:1), Beroea (17:10), Athens (17:17), Corinth (18:4), and Ephesus (18:19).

In shaking the dust off their feet (v. 51), Paul and Barnabas act on the advice Jesus gave to the Twelve (Luke 9:5) and the Seventy-two (Luke 10:10-11). And the rejoicing of the disciples in the midst of rejection and persecution acts out the fourth Beatitude of the Sermon on the Plain (Luke 6:23).

14:1-28 Paul and Barnabas, from Antioch to Antioch

Before zooming in on the marvelous details of the healing of the lame man at Lystra, Luke sketches the experiences of Paul and Barnabas in Iconium to highlight what is characteristic of their mission. (Uniquely in Acts, they are called "apostles," at verse 4 and again at verse 14, probably more to acknowledge their being on a mission [13:2] than to indicate special status.) Here they draw a positive response from "a great number of Jews and Greeks [Gentiles]." As in the work of the Twelve in Jerusalem, the Lord confirms the word through signs and wonders. As in Pisidian Antioch, the response of the larger population is divided and evokes persecution from Gentiles and Jews alike.

When we come to the dramatic events at Lystra, there can be no doubt that Luke has chosen to foreground this healing by highlighting parallels with the healing done through Peter and John in Acts 3. As in the case of

faith to be healed, [10]and called out in a loud voice, "Stand up straight on your feet." He jumped up and began to walk about. [11]When the crowds saw what Paul had done, they cried out in Lycaonian, "The gods have come down to us in human form." [12]They called Barnabas "Zeus" and Paul "Hermes," because he was the chief speaker. [13]And the priest of Zeus, whose temple was at the entrance to the city, brought oxen and garlands to the gates, for he together with the people intended to offer sacrifice.

[14]The apostles Barnabas and Paul tore their garments when they heard this and rushed out into the crowd, shouting, [15]"Men, why are you doing this? We are of the same nature as you, human beings. We proclaim to you good news that you should turn from these idols to the living God, 'who made heaven and earth and sea and all that is in them.' [16]In past generations he allowed all Gentiles to go their own ways; [17]yet, in bestowing his goodness, he did not leave himself without witness, for he gave you rains from heaven and fruitful seasons, and filled you with nourishment and gladness for your hearts." [18]Even with these words, they scarcely restrained the crowds from offering sacrifice to them.

[19]However, some Jews from Antioch and Iconium arrived and won over the crowds. They stoned Paul and dragged

---

that first major healing in the life of the Jerusalem church, here we have a healing of a man born lame sitting outside a temple, done with a verbal command, and resulting not only in standing and walking but even in leaping. Both healings are interpreted as a sign of the salvation that comes through faith (3:16; 14:9). Thus the first Gentile healing matches the first Jewish healing. The work of the second great leader (Paul) is inaugurated by a healing that parallels the dramatic healing of the first great leader of the Church (Peter). And the responses are similar. As Peter and John had to deflect the adulation of the crowd in the Jerusalem Temple, so Paul and Barnabas, taken by the pagans for Zeus and Hermes, are compelled to dodge the blasphemy of having sacrifice offered to them!

The brief speech attributed to both Barnabas and Paul invokes a strategy of evangelization that has typified missionary work at its best. Instead of moving directly to the fulfillment of messianic expectations (non-existent for the pagans of Lystra), the apostles proclaim the "living God," the creator revealed in the good gifts of nature that they celebrate in their own sacrifices—the rains and the fruitful seasons. This acknowledgment of God as creator and sustainer of all life is, of course, at the heart of Jewish monotheism; now Christianity makes it a necessary foundation of its proclamation of the gospel. Appreciation of Jesus requires knowledge and acceptance of God the creator.

him out of the city, supposing that he was dead. ²⁰But when the disciples gathered around him, he got up and entered the city. On the following day he left with Barnabas for Derbe.

End of the First Mission. ²¹After they had proclaimed the good news to that city and made a considerable number of disciples, they returned to Lystra and to Iconium and to Antioch. ²²They strengthened the spirits of the disciples and exhorted them to persevere in the faith, saying, "It is necessary for us to undergo many hardships to enter the kingdom of God." ²³They appointed presbyters for them in each church and, with prayer and fasting, commended them to the Lord in whom they had put their faith. ²⁴Then they traveled through Pisidia and reached Pamphylia. ²⁵After proclaiming the word at Perga they went down to Attalia. ²⁶From there they sailed to Antioch, where they had been commended to the grace of God for the work they had now accomplished. ²⁷And when they arrived, they called the church together and reported what God had done with them and how he had opened the door of faith to the Gentiles. ²⁸Then they spent no little time with the disciples.

The would-be stoners from Iconium, joined by adversaries from Pisidian Antioch, finally catch up with the apostles in Lystra (v. 19) and manage to carry out their intentions on Paul, leaving him for dead. Supported by the disciples, he is able to return to town and to continue his mission the next day. It is a sign of their courage that they are able to act in the spirit of the motto expressed in verse 22 and circle back through the very towns from which their persecutors came. In Lystra, Iconium, and Antioch they find Christian communities large and stable enough to require the appointment of elders (presbyters) for their governance. Luke has no trouble portraying a church that is at once charismatic and prophetic, and, at the same time, requiring the structure of appointed officers (recall the conjunction of teachers and prophets among the five named at 13:1 and the appointment of *diakonoi* in chapter 6; and see the discussion of 20:17 and 28 regarding *episcopoi, presbyteroi,* and *diakonoi*).

We sense a kind of symmetry in the narrative as the apostles return to the community that commissioned them in Syrian Antioch. This first mission commenced at the beginning of chapter 13 with mention of offices (prophets and teachers), prayer and fasting, and designation of chosen persons for "the work" with a laying on of hands and a send-off. Now that mission comes to a close with mention of officers (elders) appointed and commissioned with prayer and fasting and a reference to "the work" Paul and Barnabas have now accomplished (14:22-26). Luke has been careful to show that this first mission was not so much what Paul and

15 **Council of Jerusalem.** ¹Some who had come down from Judea were instructing the brothers, "Unless you are circumcised according to the Mosaic practice, you cannot be saved." ²Because there arose no little dissension and debate by Paul and Barnabas with them, it was decided that Paul, Barnabas, and some of the others should go up to Jerusalem to the apostles and presbyters about this question. ³They were sent on their journey by the church, and passed through Phoenicia and Samaria telling of the conversion of the Gentiles, and brought great joy to all the brothers. ⁴When they arrived in Jerusalem, they were welcomed by the church, as well as by the apostles and the presbyters, and they reported what God had done with them. ⁵But some from the party of the Pharisees who had become believers stood up and said, "It is necessary to circumcise them and direct them to observe the Mosaic law."

⁶The apostles and the presbyters met together to see about this matter. ⁷After much debate had taken place, Peter got up and said to them, "My brothers, you are well aware that from early days God

Barnabas had done but "what God had done with them and how he had opened the door of faith to the Gentiles" (v. 27).

15:1-35 The "Council" of Jerusalem. The early church resolves its first big crisis: must Gentile converts become Jews?

This account of the early church responding to and resolving its first major crisis displays at its best Luke's genius as a historian. If you have ever been a part of a leadership committee, recall a time when that group met to resolve a major policy issue. No doubt that process entailed more than one meeting, and those meetings took hours before all sides of the issue were voiced. Full resolution and implementation likely required more hours of meeting, debate, and work.

By analogy with that contemporary experience, consider what the fledgling church was facing at this point and how Luke describes its response. Becoming disciples of Jesus as the Christ had been largely a Jewish matter. It was natural, then, for the Jewish Christians to expect Gentile converts to do what Gentile converts had always done, namely, undergo circumcision (for males) and keep the full 613 laws of Moses. Obviously, those who had specialized in teaching and living the Torah, like the converts who belonged to the party of the Pharisees, would be inclined to see it this way. Others, however, such as Paul and Barnabas, who were more broadly experienced in what God had been doing among the Gentiles, were convinced that a Gentile should not have to become a Jew to become a Christian.

69

made his choice among you that through my mouth the Gentiles would hear the word of the gospel and believe. [8]And God, who knows the heart, bore witness by granting them the holy Spirit just as he did us. [9]He made no distinction between us and them, for by faith he purified their hearts. [10]Why, then, are you now putting God to the test by placing on the shoulders of the disciples a yoke that neither our ancestors nor we have been able to bear? [11]On the contrary, we believe that we are saved through the grace of the Lord Jesus, in the same way as they." [12]The whole assembly fell silent, and they listened while Paul and Barnabas described the signs and wonders God had worked among the Gentiles through them.

James on Dietary Law. [13]After they had fallen silent, James responded, "My brothers, listen to me. [14]Symeon has described how God first concerned himself with acquiring from among the

---

Remarkably, Luke manages to present the resolution of this crisis in a passage that takes only five minutes to read! In thirty-five verses, our author cuts to the essence of the matter and, in the telling of it, provides a paradigm of ecclesial decision-making that has subsequently characterized the church at its best.

Verses 1-2 present the "state of the question": visitors from the Jerusalem headquarters challenge the lenient practice of the Antioch community (not requiring circumcision of male Gentile converts), and Paul and Barnabas promptly oppose the Jerusalem people. (Although Luke does not mention Peter at this point, this confrontation could well be the altercation that Paul himself describes, for another purpose than Luke's, in Galatians 2:11-14. This is one way of reconciling the accounts of Acts 15 and Galatians 2.)

Recognizing that this is an issue that needs to be resolved at a higher level, the local church sends Paul, Barnabas, and some other representatives to Jerusalem. Their trip up to Jerusalem ("up" because topographically one always goes *up* to Jerusalem even when the trip is a north-south journey) is punctuated by their regaling the disciples with stories of the conversion of the Gentiles. Though the Antiochene party is graciously received, the Pharisee Christians firmly restate their position: Gentile converts must get circumcised and observe the Mosaic Law.

Since the Antioch delegation is meeting with "the apostles and presbyters [elders]," this is not a plenary session of the whole church but a leadership meeting. As any recorder of minutes will recognize, the phrase "after much debate had taken place" saves Luke an enormous amount of ink and parchment. Then Luke has Peter get up and retell what we who have read Acts 10 and 11 recognize as the story of Cornelius and his

Gentiles a people for his name. ¹⁵The words of the prophets agree with this, as is written:

¹⁶'After this I shall return
and rebuild the fallen hut of David;
from its ruins I shall rebuild it
and raise it up again,
¹⁷so that the rest of humanity may seek out the Lord,
even all the Gentiles on whom my name is invoked.
Thus says the Lord who accomplishes these things,
¹⁸known from of old.'

¹⁹It is my judgment, therefore, that we ought to stop troubling the Gentiles who turn to God, ²⁰but tell them by letter to avoid pollution from idols, unlawful marriage, the meat of strangled animals, and blood. ²¹For Moses, for generations now, has had those who proclaim him in every town, as he has been read in the synagogues every sabbath."

Letter of the Apostles. ²²Then the apostles and presbyters, in agreement with the whole church, decided to choose representatives and to send

household. This time the words of Peter highlight new dimensions of that experience. He says that God purified their hearts by faith, alluding to Ezekiel 36:25-26. He argues that God's endowment of the holy Spirit upon those Gentiles shows that salvation comes by "the grace of the Lord Jesus" (v. 11). The argument against the Jerusalem policy is clinched with Paul and Barnabas describing the "signs and wonders God had worked among the Gentiles through them," which we readers recognize as a reference to the events narrated in Acts 13–14.

The clincher comes, surprisingly, from the mouth of James, the leader of the Jerusalem church, that is, the one we would most expect to support the "conservative" policy of circumcising Gentile converts. His argument turns out to be a *pesher*, that is, an application of Scripture to current events, such as we have met in the speeches of Peter and the one of Paul in Pisidian Antioch. James finds confirmation of the position represented by Paul and Barnabas in the Greek version of Amos 9:11-12.

As in the case of the other *peshers*, the interpretation here requires the Greek version (Septuagint) of the prophet. This part of Amos 9 is about the restoration of Israel. But where the Hebrew text has *edom* (Edom), the Septuagint translator has read *'adam* (humanity), so that a statement about the conquest of a remnant of Edom becomes one about "the rest of humanity" seeking the Lord. How does James (or Luke) find in this passage from the Greek Bible an affirmation of an unhindered mission to the Gentiles? It reflects the same two-stage mission that the early community found in Isaiah 49:5-6, namely, (1) restoration of the tribes of Israel ("the fallen hut of David") and (2) the reception of the Gentiles ("the rest of humanity").

them to Antioch with Paul and Barnabas. The ones chosen were Judas, who was called Barsabbas, and Silas, leaders among the brothers. ²³This is the letter delivered by them: "The apostles and the presbyters, your brothers, to the brothers in Antioch, Syria, and Cilicia of Gentile origin: greetings. ²⁴Since we have heard that some of our number [who went out] without any mandate from us have upset you with their teachings and disturbed your peace of mind, ²⁵we have with one accord decided to choose representatives and to send them to you along with our beloved Barnabas and Paul, ²⁶who have dedicated their lives to the name of our Lord Jesus Christ. ²⁷So we are sending Judas and Silas who will also convey this same message by word of mouth: ²⁸'It is the decision of the holy Spirit and of us not to place on you any burden beyond these necessities, ²⁹namely, to abstain from meat sacrificed to idols, from blood, from meats of strangled animals, and from unlawful marriage. If you keep free of these, you will be doing what is right. Farewell.' "

Delegates at Antioch. ³⁰And so they were sent on their journey. Upon their arrival in Antioch they called the assembly together and delivered the letter. ³¹When the people read it, they were delighted with the exhortation. ³²Judas and Silas, who were themselves prophets, exhorted and strengthened the brothers with many words. ³³After they had spent some time there, they

---

James's solution is to acknowledge that the mission to the Gentiles is God's will but also to maintain some continuity with the past by insisting that they should require from Gentile converts what Israel had always required of resident aliens, as spelled out in Leviticus 17-18. As a sign that they are joining a community with Israelite roots, Gentile converts should follow the usual rules for resident aliens and "abstain from meat sacrificed to idols, from blood, from meats of strangled animals, and from unlawful marriage" (v. 29). (Alternatively, a convincing case can also be made that the issue here was not so much menu as venue, that the four items of the apostolic decree referred simply to the behavior involved in participating in pagan temple feasts, and that Gentile believers were hereby warned to make a clean break from such places.)

Notice that Luke's crisp account of what must have been a more extended process provides a paradigm for problem solving and decision-making in the church. It comes down to three movements:

1. Conduct a full hearing of the community's experience of what they understand God to be doing among them (here, the accounts of Peter, Paul, and Barnabas).

2. Try to understand that experience against the faith-community's tradition as currently understood (here, James's citation of Greek Amos 9).

The Temple of Athena in Athens

were sent off with greetings of peace from the brothers to those who had commissioned them. [34] 35But Paul and Barnabas remained in Antioch, teaching and proclaiming with many others the word of the Lord.

V. The Mission of Paul to the Ends of the Earth

Paul and Barnabas Separate. 36After some time, Paul said to Barnabas, "Come, let us make a return visit to see how the brothers are getting on in all the cities where we proclaimed the word of the Lord." 37Barnabas wanted to take with them also John, who was called Mark, 38but Paul insisted that they should not take with them someone who had deserted them at Pamphylia and who had not continued with them in their work. 39So sharp was their disagreement that they separated. Barnabas took Mark and sailed to Cyprus. 40But Paul chose Silas and departed after being commended by the brothers to the grace of the Lord. 41He traveled through Syria and Cilicia bringing strength to the churches.

---

3. Make a practical policy decision that affirms the values evoked in steps 1 and 2 (here, the decision to free Gentile converts from unnecessary obligations, but requiring them at least to keep the Levitical rules for resident aliens—or, on the alternative interpretation, to cease frequenting pagan temple feasts).

This very human problem-solving process is something that the community can boldly describe with the words "It is the decision of the holy Spirit and of us . . ." (v. 28).

THE MISSION OF PAUL TO THE ENDS OF THE EARTH

Acts 15:36–28:31

The travels described in Acts 16–20 cover two more distinct journeys, the second and third missionary journeys of Paul (and companions). And each journey has a distinct geographical center of gravity: as the first addressed communities in southern Galatia, the second concentrates on major cities in Macedonia and Achaia, and the third centers in, and radiates from, the great Ephesus.

Like the first journey described in chapters 13–14, the second and third also begin and return to Syrian Antioch and include one major speech by Paul—the only address to a Gentile audience (in Athens, 17:22-31) and the farewell address at Miletus to the Ephesian elders (20:18-35). Yet because these two journeys are separated by what is only a brief return to Syrian Antioch (18:22), it may be helpful (and even more faithful to Luke's narrative) to think of the activities recounted in these five chapters as the

16

Paul in Lycaonia: Timothy. [1]He reached [also] Derbe and Lystra where there was a disciple named Timothy, the son of a Jewish woman who was a believer, but his father was a Greek. [2]The brothers in Lystra and Iconium spoke highly of him, [3]and Paul wanted him to come along with him. On account of the Jews of that region, Paul had him circumcised, for they all knew that his father was a Greek. [4]As they traveled from city to city, they handed on to the people for observance the decisions reached by the apostles and presbyters in Jerusalem. [5]Day after day the churches grew stronger in faith and increased in number.

Through Asia Minor. [6]They traveled through the Phrygian and Galatian territory because they had been

Aegean mission. Together, these travels form a whole, moving from what Paul himself refers to as "the beginning of the gospel" at Philippi (Phil 4:15) to Paul's "last will and testament" addressed to the Ephesian elders at Miletus (Act 20:17-38). The remainder of the book (Acts 21–28) is a distinct segment devoted to journeys related to Paul's Jewish and Roman imprisonment and "trials" (really hearings) in Jerusalem and Caesarea Maritima, and finally house arrest in Rome.

15:36-41 Paul and Barnabas separate

Luke's delicate treatment of the interplay between the human intentions and divine will continues to unfold dramatically. What will eventually become Paul's greatest missionary expansion begins simply with the intention of revisiting and strengthening the churches he had founded in the first mission (Acts 13–14). That God can work with the results of human frailty is implied in Luke's notice that Paul and Barnabas had a "disagreement" (whose depth is suggested by the Greek word here, *paroxysmos*, v. 38, from which the English "paroxysm" derives) about whether Mark, who had deserted the previous mission at Pamphylia, should be allowed to accompany them. Thus the breakup of the first team leads to the formation of a powerful new team—Paul and Silas. First introduced in verses 22-32 as a leader in the Jerusalem community and a prophet, Silas is usually taken to be the same person as the Silvanus mentioned in the New Testament epistles.

16:1-5 Timothy joins Paul and Silas

This brief passage shows Paul's nuanced approach to Jewish/Gentile relations in the Christian mission. Even as he continues to promulgate the apostolic decree of the Council of Jerusalem (15:23-29), which frees Gentile converts from having to become Jews, he can still insist that Timothy

prevented by the holy Spirit from preaching the message in the province of Asia. [7]When they came to Mysia, they tried to go on into Bithynia, but the Spirit of Jesus did not allow them, [8]so they crossed through Mysia and came down to Troas. [9]During [the] night Paul had a vision. A Macedonian stood before him and implored him with these words, "Come over to Macedonia and help us." [10]When he had seen the vision, we sought passage to Macedonia at once, concluding that God had called us to proclaim the good news to them.

Into Europe. [11]We set sail from Troas, making a straight run for Samothrace, and on the next day to Neapolis, [12]and from there to Philippi, a leading city in that district of Macedonia and a Roman colony. We spent some time in that city. [13]On the sabbath we went outside the city gate along the river where we thought there would be a place of prayer. We sat and spoke with the women who had gathered there. [14]One of them, a woman named Lydia, a dealer in purple cloth, from the city of Thyatira, a worshiper of God, listened, and the Lord opened her heart

---

undergo adult circumcision. Apparently Timothy was raised Jewish by his mother (named Eunice, we learn in 2 Timothy 1:5) but had never been circumcised (prevented by his Greek father?). That Paul convinced him to get circumcised, even though he was now a Christian, suggests that Paul still considered mission to Jews important enough to take this surprising step to make Timothy more acceptable to his fellow Jews.

16:6-10 The call to Macedonia

The movement of this team of three into fresh mission territory presents again the delicate interface of the divine and human in their decision-making. As they move westward, they are prevented from moving south by the holy Spirit and from moving north by "the Spirit of Jesus." When Paul receives a dream vision of a Macedonian calling for help, that call still requires ratification by human decision (v. 10).

A note on the "we" passages

The introduction of the first person plural ("we") in verse 10 signals the first of the famous four "we" sections in Acts (16:10-17; 20:5-15; 21:1-18; 27:1–28:16). To account for this phenomenon, commentators have noted that the first person plural was sometimes used in ancient travel narratives as a literary device to evoke immediacy. However, this does not appear to be the case with Acts, a work of history. The abruptness of the shifts from third-person narrative to first-person (and back again) is more easily accounted for as deriving from the actual involvement of the author (or his sources). Moreover, ancient historians were eager to indicate their presence

to pay attention to what Paul was saying. [15]After she and her household had been baptized, she offered us an invitation, "If you consider me a believer in the Lord, come and stay at my home," and she prevailed on us.

Imprisonment at Philippi. [16]As we were going to the place of prayer, we met a slave girl with an oracular spirit, who used to bring a large profit to her owners through her fortune-telling. [17]She began to follow Paul and us, shouting, "These people are slaves of the Most High God, who proclaim to you a way of salvation." [18]She did this for many days. Paul became annoyed, turned, and said to the spirit, "I command you in the name of Jesus Christ to come out of her." Then it came out at that moment.

[19]When her owners saw that their hope of profit was gone, they seized Paul and Silas and dragged them to the public square before the local authorities. [20]They brought them before the magistrates and said, "These people are Jews and are disturbing our city [21]and are advocating customs that are not lawful for us Romans to adopt or practice." [22]The crowd joined in the attack on them, and the magistrates had them stripped and ordered them to be beaten with rods. [23]After inflicting many blows on them, they threw them into prison and instructed the jailer to guard them securely. [24]When he re-

at the events they described when they had grounds to make such a claim. We have no evidence of their making such claims groundlessly.

16:11-15 The conversion of Lydia and her household

Seeking a Jewish house of prayer, Paul, Silas, Timothy (and Luke, if we understand "we" historically) encounter a group of women gathered by the riverside. With marvelous economy of words, Luke describes one Lydia. She is a businesswoman, a dealer in the luxury item of purple cloth, a God fearer, and wealthy enough to be mistress of a household. Such is her openness and response to Paul's sharing of the word that Luke describes it in language reminiscent of the conversion of the Emmaus pair in Luke 24:31-32: "The Lord opened her heart." Conversion and baptism lead immediately to generous hospitality. Since the missioners later return to "Lydia's house" (v. 40) after their release from prison, she may well have emerged as the leader of the first house church of Philippi (and thus the first in what will later be known as Europe).

16:16-40 Further adventures in Philippi: deliverance, imprisonment, and further deliverance

On his way to the house of prayer, Paul encounters some unsolicited and annoying advertising. A slave girl with a mantic spirit goes around

ceived these instructions, he put them in the innermost cell and secured their feet to a stake.

Deliverance from Prison. [25]About midnight, while Paul and Silas were praying and singing hymns to God as the prisoners listened, [26]there was suddenly such a severe earthquake that the foundations of the jail shook; all the doors flew open, and the chains of all were pulled loose. [27]When the jailer woke up and saw the prison doors wide open, he drew [his] sword and was about to kill himself, thinking that the prisoners had escaped. [28]But Paul shouted out in a loud voice, "Do no harm to yourself; we are all here." [29]He asked for a light and rushed in and,

trembling with fear, he fell down before Paul and Silas. [30]Then he brought them out and said, "Sirs, what must I do to be saved?" [31]And they said, "Believe in the Lord Jesus and you and your household will be saved." [32]So they spoke the word of the Lord to him and to everyone in his house. [33]He took them in at that hour of the night and bathed their wounds; then he and all his family were baptized at once. [34]He brought them up into his house and provided a meal and with his household rejoiced at having come to faith in God.

[35]But when it was day, the magistrates sent the lictors with the order, "Release those men." [36]The jailer re-

---

shouting what is in fact the truth: "These people are slaves of the Most High God, who proclaim to you a way of salvation" (v. 17). Though true enough in a Christian context, the ambiguous language would have been heard by pagans as announcing Paul and Silas as promoting a new cure in the name of the god that they promote as the top god of the pagan pantheon. When Paul puts a stop to this with a command in the name of Jesus and the woman is delivered of the oracular spirit, her exploiters, distressed by the loss of business, bring the missioners before the Roman magistrates. The charge: illegal (anti-imperial) proselytizing.

The twosome is stripped, beaten, and imprisoned. During the night an earthquake opens the jail doors and unchains the prisoners. When the jailer finds the missioners freed but still present, he responds to these portents by falling on his knees and asking, "What must I do to be saved?" And they say, "Believe in the Lord Jesus and you and your household will be saved." As in the case of Lydia, openness leads to conversion of a household, hospitality, and baptism.

When the Roman authorities realize their mistake and try to dismiss Paul and friends discreetly, Paul confronts the police. He and his men are Roman citizens, and he insists that their beating and imprisonment without trial are a miscarriage of justice that ought to be reversed, not secretly but officially. This elicits a sheepish apology from the magistrates, who

ported the[se] words to Paul, "The magistrates have sent orders that you be released. Now, then, come out and go in peace." ³⁷But Paul said to them, "They have beaten us publicly, even though we are Roman citizens and have not been tried, and have thrown us into prison. And now, are they going to release us secretly? By no means. Let them come themselves and lead us out." ³⁸The lictors reported these words to the magistrates, and they became alarmed when they heard that they were Roman citizens. ³⁹So they came and placated them, and led them out and asked that they leave the city. ⁴⁰When they had come out of the prison, they went to Lydia's house where they saw and encouraged the brothers, and then they left.

17 **Paul in Thessalonica.** ¹When they took the road through Amphipolis and Apollonia, they reached Thessalonica, where there was a synagogue of the Jews. ²Following his usual custom, Paul joined them, and for three sabbaths he entered into discussions with them from the scriptures, ³expounding and demonstrating that the Messiah had to suffer and rise from the dead, and that "This is the Messiah, Jesus, whom I proclaim to you." ⁴Some of them were convinced and joined Paul and Silas; so, too, a great number of Greeks who were worshipers, and not a few of the prominent women. ⁵But the Jews became jealous and recruited some worthless men loitering in the public square, formed a mob, and set the city in turmoil. They

come to apologize and to ask them to leave town. This they do, but not without stopping at Lydia's place to encourage the budding Philippian community.

17:1-15 From Thessalonica to Beroea, with mixed reviews

Although Luke treats Paul's mission in Thessalonica (some hundred miles west of Philippi) as a brief, three-week encounter, the community he founded there was significant enough to receive the earliest letter we have from the Apostle's hand, 1 Thessalonians.

The events here are described in language that resonates with the Third Gospel. When Luke notes that Paul joined the local synagogue community according to "his usual custom," he could be referring to Paul's usual missionary strategy. He could as well mean that Paul attended synagogue as his Jewish practice, much as Jesus attended the Nazareth synagogue "according to his custom" (Luke 4:16). His teaching in that house of prayer and study is summarized in words that reflect the message of Jesus to the disciples on Easter Sunday ("The Messiah had to suffer and rise from the dead," v. 3; see Luke 24:26, 46-47). And when those in the Jewish community who find Paul's message a threat drag to the

marched on the house of Jason, intending to bring them before the people's assembly. ⁵When they could not find them, they dragged Jason and some of the brothers before the city magistrates, shouting, "These people who have been creating a disturbance all over the world have now come here, ⁷and Jason has welcomed them. They all act in opposition to the decrees of Caesar and claim instead that there is another king, Jesus." ⁸They stirred up the crowd and the city magistrates who, upon hearing these charges, ⁹took a surety payment from Jason and the others before releasing them.

Paul in Beroea. ¹⁰The brothers immediately sent Paul and Silas to Beroea during the night. Upon arrival they went to the synagogue of the Jews. ¹¹These Jews were more fair-minded than those in Thessalonica, for they received the word with all willingness and examined the scriptures daily to determine whether these things were so. ¹²Many of them became believers, as did not a few of the influential Greek women and men. ¹³But when the Jews of Thessalonica learned that the word of God had now been proclaimed by Paul in Beroea also, they came there too to cause a commotion and stir up the crowds. ¹⁴So the brothers at once sent Paul on his way to the seacoast, while Silas and Timothy remained behind. ¹⁵After Paul's escorts had taken him to Athens, they came away with instructions for Silas and Timothy to join him as soon as possible.

Paul in Athens. ¹⁶While Paul was waiting for them in Athens, he grew exasperated at the sight of the city full of

---

magistrates some of the small Christian community growing in Jason's place, their accusations echo those leveled against Jesus: "They all act in opposition to the decrees of Caesar and claim instead that there is another king, Jesus" (v. 7; see Luke 23:2).

Some sixty miles to the southwest, Paul and Silas find a much more receptive synagogue in Beroea, where people engage the missioners in biblical study, not just on the Sabbath but "daily" (v. 11). But the zealous Thessalonian adversaries soon arrive to stir up the crowds against them, much as the pre-Christian Paul (Saul) traveled distances to block the spread of what he had determined was a dangerous Jewish heresy, "the Way" (Acts 9:2).

17:16-34 Paul in Athens

In this episode Luke presents Paul giving the only fully developed speech to a Gentile audience. He describes that audience with care when he highlights the Stoics and Epicureans in verse 18 (both named only here in the New Testament). The mere mention of the names evokes stereotyped philosophical positions regarding humanity, nature, and the gods. Stoics perceived reality as a unified, organic cosmos in which the divinity

81

The Parthenon on the Acropolis in Athens, built to give thanks to Athena, the city's patron goddess.

idols. [17]So he debated in the synagogue with the Jews and with the worshipers, and daily in the public square with whoever happened to be there. [18]Even some of the Epicurean and Stoic philosophers engaged him in discussion. Some asked, "What is this scavenger trying to say?" Others said, "He sounds like a promoter of foreign deities," because he was preaching about 'Jesus' and 'Resurrection.' [19]They took him and led him to the Areopagus and said, "May we learn what this new teaching is that you speak of? [20]For you bring some strange notions to our ears; we should like to know what these things mean." [21]Now all the Athenians as well as the foreigners residing there used their time for nothing else but telling or hearing something new.

Paul's Speech at the Areopagus. [22]Then Paul stood up at the Areopagus and said:

"You Athenians, I see that in every respect you are very religious. [23]For as I walked around looking carefully at your shrines, I even discovered an altar inscribed, 'To an Unknown God.' What therefore you unknowingly worship, I proclaim to you. [24]The God who made the world and all that is in it, the Lord of heaven and earth, does not dwell in

---

inhered pantheistically as a kind of "law." Humanity was part of that cosmos and found happiness by harmonizing with that essentially benevolent law of the cosmos.

Epicureans, on the other hand, had a more mechanistic notion of the world, in which the divine was conceived in a "deistic" way at best (the divinity causing the cosmos but remaining uninvolved with it). Epicureans expected mere dissolution after death and, meanwhile, sought happiness by prudently doing what was most sensibly pleasant. It makes sense, then, for Luke to describe the crowd reactions as divided. On the one hand, there were those who heckled Paul, dismissing him as a "seed-pecker," a reaction that fits the Epicureans, who would have found Paul's teaching radically incompatible with their own. On the other hand, there were those who were initially confused (thinking Paul to be speaking of new gods, *Iēsous* and *Anastasis* ["Resurrection," mis-heard as the name of the divine consort of *Iēsous*?]) yet remained open to the preacher and wanted to hear more. And this reaction fits the Stoics, who would have found some tantalizing convergences with their worldview and lifestyle and would have been drawn to further inquiry.

The notion that the deity is not captured in sanctuaries and does not need human worship (see 7:48) would have been congenial to Stoics and Epicureans alike. But against Stoic pantheism, Paul asserts the biblical notion of a transcendent creator who *made* everything and, moreover, sustains everything. Paul reminds them of the common origin of the human

sanctuaries made by human hands, [25]nor is he served by human hands because he needs anything. Rather it is he who gives to everyone life and breath and everything. [26]He made from one the whole human race to dwell on the entire surface of the earth, and he fixed the ordered seasons and the boundaries of their regions, [27]so that people might seek God, even perhaps grope for him and find him, though indeed he is not far from any one of us. [28]For 'In him we live and move and have our being,' as even some of your poets have said, 'For we too are his offspring.' [29]Since therefore we are the offspring of God, we ought not to think that the divinity is like an image fashioned from gold, silver, or stone by human art and imagination. [30]God has overlooked the times of ignorance, but now he demands that all people everywhere repent [31]because he has established a day on which he will 'judge the world with justice' through a man he has appointed, and he has provided confirmation for all by raising him from the dead."

[32]When they heard about resurrection of the dead, some began to scoff, but others said, "We should like to hear you on this some other time." [33]And so Paul left them. [34]But some did join him, and became believers. Among them

---

family ("made from one"—compatible with the biblical account of origin from Adam and also the fresh beginning with Noah). Echoing his brief proclamation to the Lycaonians at Lystra, Paul remodels LXX Isaiah 42:5 and calls them to contemplate the earth with its seasons as a habitat for humanity and a revelation of the Creator's care.

Where he might have cited Scripture for a synagogue audience, here Paul enlists instead an ancient Stoic poet from his region, Aratus ("for we too are his offspring"), and he also quotes a sixth-century B.C. author, Epimenides of Knossos: "In him we live and move and have our being." Thus Luke appropriates Hellenistic language to assert against Stoic pantheism what we might call a biblical panentheism. Against the Stoic notion of endless cycles of cosmic rebirth and death, he announces the biblical doomsday. Against the coldness of Epicurean "deism," he asserts the biblical notion of God's intimate involvement with creatures. If Luke has said in verse 24 that human handicraft cannot *house* God, in verse 29 he argues that human skill and wit cannot *image* the divinity. The unexpressed element of the argument is the biblical idea that the only adequate image of the living God is living human beings, who are images of the King of the universe insofar as they are stewards of the earth.

If Jesus is going to be the ultimate judge of the human family, it would follow that the criteria are what we have heard him teach in the Third Gospel, especially in the Sermon on the Plain (Luke 6:20-49).

were Dionysius, a member of the Court of the Areopagus, a woman named Damaris, and others with them.

18 **Paul in Corinth.** ¹After this he left Athens and went to Corinth. ²There he met a Jew named Aquila, a native of Pontus, who had recently come from Italy with his wife Priscilla because Claudius had ordered all the Jews to leave Rome. He went to visit them ³and, because he practiced the same trade, stayed with them and worked, for they were tentmakers by trade. ⁴Every sabbath, he entered into discussions in the synagogue, attempting to convince both Jews and Greeks.

⁵When Silas and Timothy came down from Macedonia, Paul began to occupy himself totally with preaching the word, testifying to the Jews that the Messiah was Jesus. ⁶When they opposed him and reviled him, he shook out his garments and said to them, "Your blood be on your heads! I am clear of responsibility. From now on I will go to the Gentiles." ⁷So he left there and went to a house belonging to a man named Titus Justus, a worshiper

Commentators have noted that Paul is portrayed using this philosophical "natural theology" approach just this once in Acts. And in his first letter to the Corinthians, he makes a point of not coming to them with the wisdom of philosophers but simply with the "foolishness" of a crucified Messiah. Was the approach of Paul in Athens simply a failed strategy, never to be repeated? It would seem, rather, that the church has seen in this episode a model of how Jerusalem can speak to Athens. Thomas Aquinas, for example, used the philosophical categories of a rediscovered Aristotle to speak to his European culture. And theology has always been an effort to recast the givens of revelation in the language of one's own time and place. One can even see in this brief masterpiece hints of the basis for the interreligious dialogue that challenges us today.

18:1-17 Paul in Corinth

Because the New Testament contains two of the letters that Paul later wrote to the Christian community in Corinth, we know more about this community than any of the other churches that Paul founded. The correspondence that we call 1 and 2 Corinthians gives us a privileged window on the texture and tensions of this vibrant community in the middle fifties of the first century. In the first half of Acts 18, Luke, apparently working from sources other than Paul's letters, sketches the beginnings of that fascinating church. Some of the strokes of that sketch provide precious contact with historical data; other strokes limn Luke's inspired interpretation of those events, showing what God is doing through human failures and successes in that busy crossroads of the ancient world.

of God; his house was next to a synagogue. [8]Crispus, the synagogue official, came to believe in the Lord along with his entire household, and many of the Corinthians who heard believed and were baptized. [9]One night in a vision the Lord said to Paul, "Do not be afraid. Go on speaking, and do not be silent, [10]for I am with you. No one will attack and harm you, for I have many people in this city." [11]He settled there for a year and a half and taught the word of God among them.

Accusations before Gallio. [12]But when Gallio was proconsul of Achaia, the Jews rose up together against Paul and brought him to the tribunal, [13]saying, "This man is inducing people to worship God contrary to the law." [14]When Paul was about to reply, Gallio spoke to the Jews, "If it were a matter of some crime or malicious fraud, I should with reason hear the complaint of you Jews; [15]but since it is a question of arguments over doctrine and titles and your own law, see to it yourselves. I do not wish to be a judge of such matters." [16]And he drove them away from the tribunal. [17]They all seized Sosthenes, the synagogue official, and beat him in

---

Acts 18 offers two important links with secular history. The Roman historian Suetonius tells us that the emperor Claudius expelled members of the Jewish community of Rome because of an "uproar" caused by one "Chrestus" in A.D. 49. Scholars have taken that to be a garbled reference to *Christos*. It would seem to refer to a stir caused by Jewish Christians from Jerusalem preaching Jesus as the Messiah. Priscilla and Aquila, then, seem to be part of that group expelled from Rome. They are "Jews for Jesus" who host Christian meetings at their house (1 Cor 16:19), as they will later do in Rome, when Nero allows Jews to return five years later (see Rom 16:5). This enterprising couple takes in as houseguest Paul, their fellow tentmaker and messianic missioner. An inscription found at Delphi dates the proconsul of Achaia, Gallio, to A.D. 51–52, thus providing another link to secular history.

But it is sacred history that most interests Luke. He shows that the whim of an emperor and the adjudication of a proconsul can play into the divine project. Aquila and Prisca (Priscilla) become two of Paul's principal co-workers, and their hospitality enables the Apostle to settle into what was (next to his twenty-seven-month stay in Ephesus; see 19:10) his second most extended sojourn in a single town, lasting some eighteen months.

Paul's extended sessions at the local Jewish house of study, with Gentile God-fearers as well as Jews in attendance, issue in the usual mixed results. Most Jews reject the novelty of a crucified craftsman proclaimed as the Messiah and "the Lord." But there are notable exceptions: Crispus, the synagogue leader, and one Titus Justus, the God-fearer who owned the house next door to the synagogue. Paul's work is affirmed by a night

full view of the tribunal. But none of this was of concern to Gallio.

Return to Syrian Antioch. [18]Paul remained for quite some time, and after saying farewell to the brothers he sailed for Syria, together with Priscilla and Aquila. At Cenchreae he had his hair cut because he had taken a vow. [19]When they reached Ephesus, he left them there, while he entered the synagogue and held discussions with the Jews. [20]Although they asked him to stay for a longer time, he did not consent, [21]but as he said farewell he promised, "I shall come back to you again, God willing." Then he set sail from Ephesus. [22]Upon landing at Caesarea, he went up and greeted the church and then went down to Antioch. [23]After staying there some time, he left and traveled in orderly sequence through the Galatian country and Phrygia, bringing strength to all the disciples.

Apollos. [24]A Jew named Apollos, a native of Alexandria, an eloquent speaker, arrived in Ephesus. He was an

---

vision of Jesus assuring him in language that recalls the divine promise of support to the prophets Isaiah and Jeremiah ("I am with you").

Tellingly, the mixed Christian community is called the Lord's "people" (*laos*, the biblical word for the people of the covenant; source of our word "laity"). When Paul's Jewish adversaries bring him before the bench of the proconsul Gallio, he unwittingly affirms that "covenantal peoplehood" of the Christians by dismissing their charges against Paul as a matter of Jewish doctrine, titles, and law (v. 15).

18:18-28 Further mission notes and the integration of Apollos

Luke's intent in the remainder of chapter 18 seems mainly to give a summary of activity occurring between Paul's work in Corinth and his work in another major urban center, Ephesus (to be treated in Acts 19). The résumé highlights features that are key to Luke's interpretation. (1) Paul continues to operate as a Jew (see the reference to the Nazirite haircut, v. 18; for background, see Num 6:1-21). (2) He continues his mission to fellow Jews (he dialogues with the Ephesian synagogue congregation). (3) He stays in touch with church officials at the Jerusalem headquarters (v. 22). (4) The Christian mission continues in an orderly way. For example, Paul revisits and affirms communities established in Phrygia and Galatia. And when Apollos, a skilled rhetorician from the Hellenistic Christian/Jewish community of Alexandria, arrives in Ephesus and begins to preach the "Way of the Lord" with enthusiasm, but incompletely, Paul's co-workers, Priscilla and Aquila, explain the Way to him more fully. Apollos's move from Ephesus to Achaia is done with the recommendation of the Ephesian Christians.

authority on the scriptures. ²⁵He had been instructed in the Way of the Lord and, with ardent spirit, spoke and taught accurately about Jesus, although he knew only the baptism of John. ²⁶He began to speak boldly in the synagogue; but when Priscilla and Aquila heard him, they took him aside and explained to him the Way [of God] more accurately. ²⁷And when he wanted to cross to Achaia, the brothers encouraged him and wrote to the disciples there to welcome him. After his arrival he gave great assistance to those who had come to believe through grace.

²⁸He vigorously refuted the Jews in public, establishing from the scriptures that the Messiah is Jesus.

19 **Paul in Ephesus.** ¹While Apollos was in Corinth, Paul traveled through the interior of the country and came [down] to Ephesus where he found some disciples. ²He said to them, "Did you receive the holy Spirit when you became believers?" They answered him, "We have never even heard that there is a holy Spirit." ³He said, "How were you baptized?" They replied, "With the baptism of John." ⁴Paul then said, "John baptized with a baptism of

---

(The power of Apollos's ministry was such that some of those he trains will form a kind of "I had the great Apollos as my personal trainer" faction, and Paul will have to address this issue in 1 Corinthians 1–3. See especially 1 Corinthians 3:6: "I planted, Apollos watered, but *God* caused the growth," emphasis added).

19:1-40 Paul in Ephesus: the Way of the Lord Jesus versus magic and idolatry; evangelizing from the Asian capital (19:1-12)

Paul's encounter with twelve Ephesian "disciples" who had not received the holy Spirit provides an instructive parallel with the previous episode—Priscilla and Aquila's instruction of Apollos. Both involve the instruction of disciples who are somehow incomplete. Apollos's incompleteness was subtle: although he had been instructed in the Way of the Lord (vv. 25-26; see 9:2; 14:16; 16:17) and taught accurately about Jesus and was ardent in spirit, he knew only the baptism of John, was not described as filled with the Spirit, and needed to be taught *more* accurately about the Way. Similarly, these twelve Ephesians, who seem to have missed the training of Aquila, Prisca, and the reformed Apollos, also knew only John's baptism and had not even heard that there was a holy Spirit.

As in the case of the conversion of Cornelius's household (10:44-46), a "mini-Pentecost" follows. These two descriptions of "regularizing" disciples tell us two interesting things about the emergent church: (a) that the influence of John the Baptist was more powerful than we usually give him credit for, and (b) unity of belief and practice within the church had been a struggle from the beginning.

repentance, telling the people to believe in the one who was to come after him, that is, in Jesus." [5]When they heard this, they were baptized in the name of the Lord Jesus. [6]And when Paul laid [his] hands on them, the holy Spirit came upon them, and they spoke in tongues and prophesied. [7]Altogether there were about twelve men.

[8]He entered the synagogue, and for three months debated boldly with persuasive arguments about the kingdom of God. [9]But when some in their obstinacy and disbelief disparaged the Way before the assembly, he withdrew and took his disciples with him and began to hold daily discussions in the lecture hall of Tyrannus. [10]This continued for two years with the result that all the inhabitants of the province of Asia heard the word of the Lord, Jews and Greeks alike. [11]So extraordinary were the mighty deeds God accomplished at the hands of Paul [12]that when face cloths or aprons that touched his skin were applied to the sick, their diseases left them and the evil spirits came out of them.

The Jewish Exorcists. [13]Then some itinerant Jewish exorcists tried to invoke the name of the Lord Jesus over those with evil spirits, saying, "I adjure you by the Jesus whom Paul preaches." [14]When the seven sons of Sceva, a Jewish high priest, tried to do this, [15]the evil spirit said to them in reply, "Jesus I recognize, Paul I know, but who are you?"

The summary description in verses 8-12 portrays the shape of the next twenty-seven months of Paul's evangelization. Despite past rejections, his serious effort to bring the Good News to his fellow Jews first continues with a three-month colloquium in the Ephesian synagogue. That this effort was not entirely without success is hinted at in the reference to the *disciples* whom Paul took with him after a nasty confrontation compelled him to change his venue to the hall of Tyrannus.

During the next two years Ephesus becomes a mission center from which the whole province of Asia is evangelized, "Jews and Greeks alike." The description of healings occasioned even by cloth or aprons touched to Paul's skin demonstrates that the healing ministry begun in Jesus (Luke 8:44-47, the woman with the flow of blood) and continued through Peter (Acts 5:15-16) persists in the Apostle to the Gentiles. See Paul's own reference to his work as "what Christ has accomplished through me to lead the Gentiles to obedience by word and deed, by the power of signs and wonders . . ." (Rom 15:18-19; see also 2 Cor 12:12).

19:13-20 The power of Jesus' name versus demons and magic

The power of the risen Lord Jesus over the competing powers of this world is now illustrated by two vivid and entertaining anecdotes regarding demons, magic, and idolatry.

A stone-paved street in Ephesus

¹⁶The person with the evil spirit then sprang at them and subdued them all. He so overpowered them that they fled naked and wounded from that house. ¹⁷When this became known to all the Jews and Greeks who lived in Ephesus, fear fell upon them all, and the name of the Lord Jesus was held in great esteem. ¹⁸Many of those who had become believers came forward and openly acknowledged their former practices. ¹⁹Moreover, a large number of those who had practiced magic collected their books and burned them in public. They calculated their value and found it to be fifty thousand silver pieces. ²⁰Thus did the word of the Lord continue to spread with influence and power.

Paul's Plans. ²¹When this was concluded, Paul made up his mind to travel through Macedonia and Achaia, and then to go on to Jerusalem, saying, "After I have been there, I must visit Rome also." ²²Then he sent to Macedonia two of his assistants, Timothy and Erastus, while he himself stayed for a while in the province of Asia.

The Riot of the Silversmiths. ²³About that time a serious disturbance broke out concerning the Way. ²⁴There

---

When the seven sons of the high priest Sceva attempt to deliver a man from demonic oppression by using Jesus' name in a magical way, they themselves are rebuked, overpowered, and sent packing, naked and wounded. The spiritual power of the name of the Lord Jesus, properly used, is dramatized by the immense commercial value of books burned by those converted from their magical practices (v. 19).

19:21-40 A confused assembly confronted

The Way of the Lord Jesus continues to have practical consequences. The silversmiths of Ephesus riot when their livelihood (selling silver models of the world-famous temple of the goddess Artemis) appears to be threatened by the Christian preaching against idolatry. (Archaeology helps us to picture the structures involved here. One of the "seven wonders of the ancient world," the temple of Artemis, the Artemision, was four times the size of the Parthenon, with 127 sixty-foot pillars. The dimensions alone help us understand why silver models of the place were such hot items in the religious tourism trade. And the "theater" was not like your local movie house but a magnificent amphitheater carved into a mountainside, 495 feet in diameter.) Two important points emerge from Luke's account of this disruption. First, the intervention of the town clerk models the way for Roman officials to work out tensions with Christians: ("let the matter be settled in the lawful assembly," v. 39).

Second, some of Luke's word choices hint that he is making a subtle contrast between pagan chaos and Christian order. Describing the riot,

was a silversmith named Demetrius who made miniature silver shrines of Artemis and provided no little work for the craftsmen. 25He called a meeting of these and other workers in related crafts and said, "Men, you know well that our prosperity derives from this work. 26As you can now see and hear, not only in Ephesus but throughout most of the province of Asia this Paul has persuaded and misled a great number of people by saying that gods made by hands are not gods at all. 27The danger grows, not only that our business will be discredited, but also that the temple of the great goddess Artemis will be of no account, and that she whom the whole province of Asia and all the world worship will be stripped of her magnificence."

28When they heard this, they were filled with fury and began to shout, "Great is Artemis of the Ephesians!" 29The city was filled with confusion, and the people rushed with one accord into the theater, seizing Gaius and Aristarchus, the Macedonians, Paul's traveling companions. 30Paul wanted to go before the crowd, but the disciples would not let him, 31and even some of the Asiarchs who were friends of his sent word to him advising him not to venture into the theater. 32Meanwhile, some were shouting one thing, others something else; the assembly was in chaos, and most of the people had no idea why they had come together. 33Some of the crowd prompted Alexander, as the Jews pushed him forward, and Alexander signaled with his hand

---

Luke says that the city was filled with *synchysis* ("confusion"—v. 29). Used only once in the New Testament, this is a deftly chosen word, for it is the word used in the Septuagint at Genesis 11:9 (the sole occurrence in the Greek version of the Torah) to translate the name "Babel." And Luke has already used the verbal form of the word to describe the Pentecost experience as a reversal of Babel's confusion (Acts 2:6), Pentecost being the occasion when people are confused by their ability to understand!

The contrast is further enhanced by Luke's using *ekklēsia* to describe the confused assembly in verses 32, 39, and 41. Apart from Acts 7:38, where the word refers to the assembly of the Hebrews at Sinai, *ekklēsia* elsewhere in Acts always means the community of the church. Only in this passage is the word used for a non-ecclesial assembly. For the original readers of Acts, this word choice could only have pointed up the contrast between the two kinds of "assembly"—the confused riot of the silversmiths versus the orderly growth of the church (vv. 10-17, 20). The final two occurrences of *ekklēsia* in Acts turn up in the very next chapter, in verses 17 and 28, where they describe the Ephesian church as an assembly driven by motives quite other than idolatry, greed, and anxiety.

that he wished to explain something to the gathering. [34]But when they recognized that he was a Jew, they all shouted in unison, for about two hours, "Great is Artemis of the Ephesians!" [35]Finally the town clerk restrained the crowd and said, "You Ephesians, what person is there who does not know that the city of the Ephesians is the guardian of the temple of the great Artemis and of her image that fell from the sky? [36]Since these things are undeniable, you must calm yourselves and not do anything rash. [37]The men you brought here are not temple robbers, nor have they insulted our goddess. [38]If Demetrius and his fellow craftsmen have a complaint against anyone, courts are in session, and there are proconsuls. Let them bring charges against one another. [39]If you have anything further to investigate, let the matter be settled in the lawful assembly, [40]for, as it is, we are in danger of being charged with rioting because of today's conduct. There is no cause for it. We shall [not] be able to give a reason for this demonstration." With these words he dismissed the assembly.

20 **Journey to Macedonia and Greece.** [1]When the disturbance was over, Paul had the disciples summoned and, after encouraging them, he bade them farewell and set out on his journey to Macedonia. [2]As he traveled throughout those regions, he provided many words of encouragement for them. Then he arrived in Greece, [3]where he stayed for three months. But when a plot was made against him by

20:1-16 Journeying toward Jerusalem
(and the resuscitation of "Lucky")

In a note between the episodes of the triumph over the exorcists and the riot of the silversmiths (19:21), Luke had already referred to Paul's decision to travel to Jerusalem (and then move on to Rome). Although Paul later (24:17) refers to the purpose of this journey as the bringing of alms to Jerusalem (the collection referred to in his letters to Corinth and Rome—for instance, Romans 15:25-28), there is no mention of the collection here in chapter 20. Perhaps the delivery of the Jerusalem relief fund was not the public-relations success Paul had hoped for.

After a farewell tour of churches in Macedonia and three months in "Greece" (Achaia, centering, no doubt, around unnamed Corinth), Paul, intending to join what was apparently a pilgrim group of Jews sailing for Syria, learns of a plot against him and decides to take a more indirect route, looping back around the Aegean basin. The seven names listed (plus the author or his source, since the second "we" section begins in verse 5) comprise a delegation representing most of the sectors of Paul's mission. This delegation fits the notion that this is indeed the "Jerusalem relief fund" trip (see Rom 15:25-27).

the Jews as he was about to set sail for Syria, he decided to return by way of Macedonia.

Return to Troas. ⁴Sopater, the son of Pyrrhus, from Beroea, accompanied him, as did Aristarchus and Secundus from Thessalonica, Gaius from Derbe, Timothy, and Tychicus and Trophimus from Asia ⁵who went on ahead and waited for us at Troas. ⁶We sailed from Philippi after the feast of Unleavened Bread, and rejoined them five days later in Troas, where we spent a week.

Eutychus Restored to Life. ⁷On the first day of the week when we gathered to break bread, Paul spoke to them because he was going to leave on the next day, and he kept on speaking until midnight. ⁸There were many lamps in the upstairs room where we were gathered, ⁹and a young man named Eutychus who was sitting on the window sill was sinking into a deep sleep as Paul talked on and on. Once overcome by sleep, he fell down from the third story and when he was picked up, he was dead. ¹⁰Paul went down, threw himself upon him, and said as he embraced him, "Don't be alarmed; there is life in him." ¹¹Then he returned upstairs, broke the bread, and ate; after a long conversation that lasted until daybreak, he departed. ¹²And they took the boy away alive and were immeasurably comforted.

The colorful anecdote about the resuscitation of Eutychus (aptly named "Lucky," the meaning of his name in Greek) may well be included here simply for its entertainment value and its parallel with the account of Peter's raising of Tabitha (9:36-43). But given Luke's careful choice of words and phrases—"on the first day of the week" (v. 1; see Luke 24:1); "upstairs room" (v. 8; see 1:13; 9:37, 39); "break[ing] bread" (vv. 7, 11; see Luke 22:19; 24:30; Acts 2:46); a fallen youth taken up "dead" (v. 9) and revived by Paul imitating the gestures of Elijah and Elisha and taken away as a *pais zōnta* ("living lad"), it is hard to dismiss the possibility that the author intends the reader to reflect on the story's symbolic resonances, especially when one notices that the event sits between references to Passover ("the feast of Unleavened Bread," v. 6) and Pentecost (v. 16). For the Christian practice of the breaking of the bread on the first day of the week (Sunday) is always a celebration of death and restoration to new life, precisely as these things are interpreted in the light of the Jewish feasts of Passover and Pentecost.

As for the detailed itinerary surrounding this anecdote, the listing of places could simply be explained as evidence of an eyewitness's passion for detail. It could also reflect Luke's intention to show how Jesus' heroic follower Paul imitates his master even in his making an extended final journey to Jerusalem, where he too will be interrogated by Jewish and Gentile officials.

Journey to Miletus. ¹³We went ahead to the ship and set sail for Assos where we were to take Paul on board, as he had arranged, since he was going overland. ¹⁴When he met us in Assos, we took him aboard and went on to Mitylene. ¹⁵We sailed away from there on the next day and reached a point off Chios, and a day later we reached Samos, and on the following day we arrived at Miletus. ¹⁶Paul had decided to sail past Ephesus in order not to lose time in the province of Asia, for he was hurrying to be in Jerusalem, if at all possible, for the day of Pentecost.

Paul's Farewell Speech at Miletus. ¹⁷From Miletus he had the presbyters of the church at Ephesus summoned. ¹⁸When they came to him, he addressed them, "You know how I lived among you the whole time from the day I first came to the province of Asia. ¹⁹I served the Lord with all humility and with the tears and trials that came to me because of the plots of the Jews, ²⁰and I did not at all shrink from telling you what was for your benefit, or from teaching you in public or in your homes. ²¹I earnestly bore witness for both Jews and Greeks to repentance before God and to faith

20:17-38 Paul's testament to the Ephesian elders

Paul makes a point of bypassing Ephesus (to avoid those plotting against him?), but he is eager to summon the elders of that community to Miletus, some forty miles to the south, so that he can bid them farewell. What follows is the only speech in Acts that Paul addresses to a Christian audience.

The speech follows the conventions of other biblical testaments, touching on the topics of a review of the speaker's life, commissioning of successors, encouragement and warnings regarding the future, farewell and blessing. Like other classic farewell addresses, it serves both to present the speaker as a model for the readers/auditors and also to address the historical aftermath of the speaker and interpret what is going forward historically.

In the context of Luke-Acts, the speech is a privileged moment in Paul's own imitation of Christ. Like Jesus, he makes his own "passion prediction" on the way to Jerusalem. And his farewell address to the Ephesian elders has much in common with Jesus' own farewell address to the apostles at the Last Supper (Luke 22:25-38). Like Jesus at the supper, Paul characterizes authority in the messianic community as one of humble service, focuses on the kingdom, encourages his listeners to care for those left in their charge (Jesus: "Strengthen your brothers"; Paul: "Help the weak"), and warns of future challenges. That Paul can serve as model to the extent that he himself has imitated Jesus is suggested by explicit reference to Jesus in the beatitude that climaxes the speech: "It is more blessed to give than to receive" (v. 35).

in our Lord Jesus. [22]But now, compelled by the Spirit, I am going to Jerusalem. What will happen to me there I do not know, [23]except that in one city after another the holy Spirit has been warning me that imprisonment and hardships await me. [24]Yet I consider life of no importance to me, if only I may finish my course and the ministry that I received from the Lord Jesus, to bear witness to the gospel of God's grace.

[25]"But now I know that none of you to whom I preached the kingdom during my travels will ever see my face again. [26]And so I solemnly declare to you this day that I am not responsible for the blood of any of you, [27]for I did not shrink from proclaiming to you the entire plan of God. [28]Keep watch over yourselves and over the whole flock of which the holy Spirit has appointed you overseers, in which you tend the church of God that he acquired with his own blood. [29]I know that after my departure savage wolves will come among you, and they will not spare the flock. [30]And from your own group, men will come forward perverting the truth to draw the disciples away after them. [31]So be vigilant and remember that for three years, night and day, I unceasingly admonished each of you with tears. [32]And now I commend you to God and to that gracious word of his ▶

Several things about the language of this speech are worth noting. Along with Luke's calling the group "presbyters" (*presbyteroi*, or "elders," v. 17), the usual term in Acts for leaders other than the apostles in the churches, Paul calls them "overseers" (v. 28, translating *episkopoi*, the word rendered "bishops" in later Christian writings). This reflects the apparent equivalence of those terms as found, for example, in Titus 1:5-7. In the ordinary Greek of the day, *episkopos* meant "superintendent" or "guardian" in any of a variety of social settings. In first-century Christian writings it serves as a Hellenistic equivalent of the more Judean term "elder," which Luke uses for both Jewish and Christian leaders throughout Luke-Acts. In the second century these terms will be used to designate distinct roles in the evolving three-tier hierarchical structure of a single local bishop (*episkopos*), directing a number of elders (*presbyteroi*, from which the English words "priest" and "presbyterate" derive), supported by a further group of *diakonoi*, or deacons.

One remarkable verse (v. 28) deserves special attention: "Keep watch over yourselves and over the whole flock of which the holy Spirit has appointed you overseers, in which you tend the church of God that he acquired with his own blood." This translation, which renders straightforwardly what scholars generally agree is the best reading of the Greek text, raises the question of what it can mean to speak of God's blood. An early response to this problem was the introduction of the variant reading

that can build you up and give you the inheritance among all who are consecrated. ³³I have never wanted anyone's silver or gold or clothing. ³⁴You know well that these very hands have served my needs and my companions. ³⁵In every way I have shown you that by hard work of that sort we must help the weak, and keep in mind the words of the Lord Jesus who himself said, 'It is more blessed to give than to receive.' "

³⁶When he had finished speaking he knelt down and prayed with them all. ³⁷They were all weeping loudly as they threw their arms around Paul and kissed him, ³⁸for they were deeply distressed that he had said that they would never see his face again. Then they escorted him to the ship.

21 **Arrival at Tyre.** ¹When we had taken leave of them we set sail, made a straight run for Cos, and on the next day for Rhodes, and from there to Patara. ²Finding a ship crossing to Phoenicia, we went on board and put out to sea. ³We caught sight of Cyprus but passed by it on our left and sailed on toward Syria and put in at Tyre where the ship was to unload cargo. ⁴There we sought out the disciples and stayed for a

---

"church of the Lord" for "church of God," which was open to the understanding that "his blood" referred to the blood of the Lord Jesus. But the more difficult reading, "church of God," does appear to be the more authentic one. A possible solution of this crux is to translate the final phrase, "the blood of his Own" (referring to the Son, Jesus). In any case, with the references to "holy Spirit," "God," and "blood," we have in this verse a rare New Testament adumbration of the later, more developed doctrine of the Trinity. Using phrases that catch important aspects of Paul's theology as it is expressed in the Pauline letters (conversion to God, faith in the Lord Jesus, the power of the Spirit to form community, the gospel of God's grace, the plan of God, the importance of perseverance), this speech is a fitting conclusion to Luke's narrative of Paul's intra-Christian ministry.

21:1-14 Paul and the delegation continue the journey to Jerusalem

After departing from Ephesus, Paul and companions continue the journey to Jerusalem. This stage of the journey comprises the third "we" section in Acts (vv. 1-18), implying the author's presence during this part of the journey. The summary gives us a glimpse of how people got about the Mediterranean in those days: they hung around a port until they found a cargo ship going in the general direction of their intended destination.

The fact that Paul and his entourage find communities of Christians in Tyre and Ptolemais indicates that the evangelization of Phoenicia, to which Luke referred in 11:19, took root and flourished. Indeed, the intensity of communion with the disciples at Ptolemais is enough to warrant

week. They kept telling Paul through the Spirit not to embark for Jerusalem. ⁵At the end of our stay we left and resumed our journey. All of them, women and children included, escorted us out of the city, and after kneeling on the beach to pray, ⁶we bade farewell to one another. Then we boarded the ship, and they returned home.

Arrival at Ptolemais and Caesarea. ⁷We continued the voyage and came from Tyre to Ptolemais, where we greeted the brothers and stayed a day with them. ⁸On the next day we resumed the trip and came to Caesarea, where we went to the house of Philip the evangelist, who was one of the Seven, and stayed with him. ⁹He had four virgin daughters gifted with prophecy. ¹⁰We had been there several days when a prophet named Agabus came down from Judea. ¹¹He came up to us, took Paul's belt, bound his own feet and hands with it, and said, "Thus says the holy Spirit: This is the way the Jews will bind the owner of this belt in Jerusalem, and they will hand him over to the Gentiles." ¹²When we heard this, we and the local residents begged him not to go up to Jerusalem. ¹³Then Paul replied, "What are you doing, weeping and breaking my heart? I am prepared not only to be bound but even to die in Jerusalem for the name of the Lord

the same kind of prayerful seaside send-off they received at Ephesus (20:36-38).

These episodes illustrate that hearing and following the Spirit are not a simple matter. Although the Tyrian Christians keep telling Paul "through the Spirit" not to embark for Jerusalem, he continues. Obviously, he feels they have misinterpreted the Spirit in this case. And when Agabus, who prophesied accurately the famine during the reign of Claudius (Acts 11:28), acts out symbolically what he perceives to be the Spirit's message regarding Paul's fate in Jerusalem, he gets it only partly right: Paul will indeed be bound in Jerusalem, but by Romans, not by Jews. Faced with Paul's determination to go to Jerusalem even if it means death, it is the companions, not Paul, who imitate Jesus' struggle in facing the prospect of death (Luke 22:39-42), first with resistance, then acceptance.

21:15-26 Paul has his Jewish fidelity challenged

When Paul and company arrive in Jerusalem, James and a plenary session of the Jerusalem elders hear Paul's report about what God has been doing through his ministry among the Gentiles. The Jerusalem Christian authorities are happy enough with that good news, but they inform Paul that the success among the Gentiles has raised concerns among the "many thousands" (v. 20) of Jewish Christians in the area who have gotten the idea that he is urging all the Jews in the Diaspora to abandon the Mosaic

Jesus." [14]Since he would not be dissuaded we let the matter rest, saying, "The Lord's will be done."

Paul and James in Jerusalem. [15]After these days we made preparations for our journey, then went up to Jerusalem. [16]Some of the disciples from Caesarea came along to lead us to the house of Mnason, a Cypriot, a disciple of long standing, with whom we were to stay. [17]When we reached Jerusalem the brothers welcomed us warmly. [18]The next day, Paul accompanied us on a visit to James, and all the presbyters were present. [19]He greeted them, then proceeded to tell them in detail what God had accomplished among the Gentiles through his ministry. [20]They praised God when they heard it but said to him, "Brother, you see how many thousands of believers there are from among the Jews, and they are all zealous observers of the law. [21]They have been informed that you are teaching all the Jews who live among the Gentiles to abandon Moses and that you are telling them not to circumcise their children or to observe their customary practices. [22]What is to be done? They will surely hear that you have arrived. [23]So do what we tell you. We have four men who have taken a vow. [24]Take these men and purify yourself with them, and pay their expenses that they may have their heads shaved. In this way everyone will know that there

practices. Although nothing we have read in Acts supports this charge, Paul's own letter to the Romans shows that the notion that he was denigrating the Mosaic Law was prevalent enough to warrant the full-scale defense that he makes in that major letter.

James's strategy for damage control in this regard—having Paul accompany four men to the temple and sponsor the ceremonies fulfilling their nazirite vows (see Num 6:3-20 for the nazirite ritual)— seems promising. Twentieth-century digs to the south of the Temple Mount have revealed the *mikvaot* (immersion baths), where pilgrims ritually purified themselves before climbing the stairs leading up into the temple precincts. The public nature of this purification, along with Paul's sponsoring of the sacrifices (twelve animals, three apiece for four men) would offer a clear rebuttal to the accusations that Paul was discouraging observance of the Torah.

The reference in verse 25 to the policy regarding Gentile converts expressed in the apostolic decree of the Jerusalem Council (Acts 15:23-29) strikes an odd note here. Paul, after all, played a major part in that meeting and, indeed, helped promulgate its policy regarding Gentile converts (16:4). But the notice serves to remind the reader that the present issue, Paul's attitude toward Jewish observance of the Torah, is something other than what is expected of Gentile Christians.

is nothing to the reports they have been given about you but that you yourself live in observance of the law. ²⁵As for the Gentiles who have come to believe, we sent them our decision that they abstain from meat sacrificed to idols, from blood, from the meat of strangled animals, and from unlawful marriage." ²⁶So Paul took the men, and on the next day after purifying himself together with them entered the temple to give notice of the day when the purification would be completed and the offering made for each of them.

Paul's Arrest. ²⁷When the seven days were nearly completed, the Jews from the province of Asia noticed him in the temple, stirred up the whole crowd, and laid hands on him, ²⁸shouting, "Fellow Israelites, help us. This is the man who is teaching everyone everywhere against the people and the law and this place, and what is more, he has even brought Greeks into the temple and defiled this sacred place." ²⁹For they had previously seen Trophimus the Ephesian in the city with him and supposed that Paul had brought him into the temple. ³⁰The whole city was in turmoil with people rushing together. They seized Paul and dragged him out of the temple, and immediately the gates were closed. ³¹While they were trying to kill him, a

---

Given Paul's own language about "[dying] to the law" (Gal 2:19), some commentators find Luke's portrayal here of Paul's "compromise" implausible. Yet it can be argued that Paul is acting in a way wholly consistent with the policy he articulates in 1 Corinthians 9:19-21: "Although I am free in regard to all, I have made myself a slave to all so as to win over as many as possible. To the Jews I became like a Jew to win over Jews; to those under the law I became like one under the law—though I myself am not under the law—to win over those under the law. To those outside the law I became like one outside the law—though I am not outside God's law but within the law of Christ—to win over those outside the law."

Sadly, in the end the strategy fails, for in the events that follow, nothing indicates that Paul's Jerusalem relief fund was accepted, and no one in the Jerusalem Christian community comes to his rescue in the confrontation that continues to unfold. The Jerusalem church, so robustly present in the early chapters of Acts and now grown to "many thousands," disappears from view during the final seven chapters.

21:27-36 Romans rescue Paul from an attempted lynching

In addition to the local members of the sect of the Nazarene, other Jews, pilgrims from the province of Asia, mount an attack against Paul. Having recognized their fellow provincial, the Gentile Trophimus, some had jumped to the conclusion that Paul had taken this man into the court

report reached the cohort commander that all Jerusalem was rioting. ³²He immediately took soldiers and centurions and charged down on them. When they saw the commander and the soldiers they stopped beating Paul. ³³The cohort commander came forward, arrested him, and ordered him to be secured with two chains; he tried to find out who he might be and what he had done. ³⁴Some in the mob shouted one thing, others something else; so, since he was unable to ascertain the truth because of the uproar, he ordered Paul to be brought into the compound. ³⁵When he reached the steps, he was carried by the soldiers because of the violence of the mob, ³⁶for a crowd of people followed and shouted, "Away with him!"

³⁷Just as Paul was about to be taken into the compound, he said to the cohort commander, "May I say something to you?" He replied, "Do you speak Greek? ³⁸So then you are not the Egyptian who started a revolt some time ago and led the four thousand assassins into the desert?" ³⁹Paul answered, "I am a Jew, of Tarsus in Cilicia, a citizen of no mean city; I request you to permit me to speak to the people." ⁴⁰When he had given his permission, Paul stood on the steps and motioned with his hand to the people; and when all was quiet he addressed them in Hebrew.

---

of Israel on the Temple Mount, thereby breaching the barrier separating Gentiles from the space reserved for Israelites. Signs posted on the balustrade forbade Gentiles to pass this point on pain of death. The rioting crowd falls upon Paul, haul him out of the sacred space, and try to kill him on the spot.

At this point the cohort commander intervenes with centurions and soldiers, who bring him to "the compound," a reference to the Antonia fortress, the military headquarters and barracks contiguous with the northwest corner of the temple platform. The shout of the crowd—"Away with him!"—echoes the cry at the trial of Jesus before Pilate (Luke 23:18).

21:37-40 Paul identifies himself

When Paul identifies himself as a Jew and a Roman citizen to the cohort commander, the latter is relieved that he is not "the Egyptian"—the last rabble-rouser the Romans had to deal with. The reference fits Josephus's account of an "Egyptian false prophet" who, a few years earlier, had led thirty thousand (Josephus's number) to the Mount of Olives to wait for Jerusalem to fall like Jericho in the days of Joshua. Paul and his purpose are something else entirely, as his ensuing speech will reveal. Having spoken to the commander in Greek, the *lingua franca* of that part of the empire, he now proceeds to address the crowd in what Luke calls "Hebrew"—almost certainly a reference to Aramaic, the mother tongue of Jesus and the common language of Judea.

22 **Paul's Defense before the Jerusalem Jews.** [1]"My brothers and fathers, listen to what I am about to say to you in my defense." [2]When they heard him addressing them in Hebrew they became all the more quiet. And he continued, [3]"I am a Jew, born in Tarsus in Cilicia, but brought up in this city. At the feet of Gamaliel I was educated strictly in our ancestral law and was zealous for God, just as all of you are today. [4]I persecuted this Way to death, binding both men and women and delivering them to prison. [5]Even the high priest and the whole council of elders can testify on my behalf. For from them I even received letters to the brothers and set out for Damascus to bring back to Jerusalem in chains for punishment those there as well.

[6]"On that journey as I drew near to Damascus, about noon a great light from the sky suddenly shone around me. [7]I fell to the ground and heard a voice saying to me, 'Saul, Saul, why are you persecuting me?' [8]I replied, 'Who are you, sir?' And he said to me, 'I am Jesus the Nazorean whom you are persecuting.' [9]My companions saw the light but did not hear the voice of the one who spoke to me. [10]I asked, 'What shall I do, sir?' The Lord answered me, 'Get up and go into Damascus, and there you will be told about everything appointed for you to do.' [11]Since I could see nothing because of the brightness of that light, I was led by hand by my companions and entered Damascus.

[12]"A certain Ananias, a devout observer of the law, and highly spoken of

22:1-21 Paul's first defense speech

Paul's exchange with the cohort commander had raised questions of ethnicity and status. Paul is a Jew, not "the Egyptian." He speaks Greek as well as Aramaic. And he is a Roman citizen. Now as he begins his speech, he makes it clear that he speaks as a Jew to Jews ("My brothers and fathers"). The clause "what I am about to say in my defense" renders the word *apologia,* the classical term for a legal defense, thereby setting the agenda for the final seven chapters of Acts. Facing a crowd driven by the zeal for the Mosaic Law—who are attacking Paul because they think he has violated that Law—he makes the perfect move to win their good will. He displays his Jewish pedigree, citing his Jewish upbringing, his training in the Law, even describing his own past persecution of "this Way" as stemming from precisely the "zeal . . . for God" that they are presently demonstrating in their persecution of him.

Just as Luke repeated twice the story of Peter's first mission to Gentiles in his encounter with Cornelius's household (in Acts 10, 11, and 15), so he retells the story of Paul's conversion/commission here, for the second in what will be another series of three accounts. No clumsy redundancy, these repetitions are the author's way of underscoring the importance of

by all the Jews who lived there, [13]came to me and stood there and said, 'Saul, my brother, regain your sight.' And at that very moment I regained my sight and saw him. [14]Then he said, 'The God of our ancestors designated you to know his will, to see the Righteous One, and to hear the sound of his voice; [15]for you will be his witness before all to what you have seen and heard. [16]Now, why delay? Get up and have yourself baptized and your sins washed away, calling upon his name.'

[17]"After I had returned to Jerusalem and while I was praying in the temple, I fell into a trance [18]and saw the Lord saying to me, 'Hurry, leave Jerusalem at once, because they will not accept your testimony about me.' [19]But I replied, 'Lord, they themselves know that from synagogue to synagogue I used to imprison and beat those who believed in you. [20]And when the blood of your witness Stephen was being shed, I myself stood by giving my approval and keeping guard over the cloaks of his murderers.' [21]Then he said to me, 'Go, I shall send you far away to the Gentiles.' "

Paul Imprisoned. [22]They listened to him until he said this, but then they

these pivotal events. As in the case of Peter's encounter with Cornelius, each retelling comes with variations and developments that fit the immediate context and help the reader fathom the significance more deeply.

In this version of Paul's encounter with the risen Jesus, the brightness is enhanced: at the most brilliant time of day, *noon*, Paul experiences a brightness that outshines the noontime sunlight! His visual impairment is not called blindness here but is simply ascribed to the brightness of the light. Whereas in the account of Acts 9 the companions heard the voice but see no one, here they see the light but hear no voice.

These are not the discrepancies of a negligent author but variations of an artist in full control of his material. Saying that "the Lord" answered Paul enhances the nature of the vision as a theophany, that is, a manifestation of God . (It is not impossible that Luke's emphasis on blindness in the midst of brightness is prompted by his perception that Paul here experiences the noontime blindness that Deuteronomy 28:28 promises Israel if it does not hearken to the voice of the Lord.)

The Jewishness of Ananias is enhanced. He is a "devout observer of the law" (v. 12). And he announces that their ancestral God has designated Paul to witness (what he had seen and heard) "before *all*" (emphasis added) about "the Righteous One," an eminently Jewish title for Jesus, denoting fidelity to the covenant and echoing Luke's unique version of the confession of the centurion under the cross (Luke 23:47: "This man was *dikaios*" ["innocent," "righteous"]). Here there is less emphasis on the physical cure from blindness; restored vision simply follows upon Ananias's word.

raised their voices and shouted, "Take such a one as this away from the earth. It is not right that he should live." ²³And as they were yelling and throwing off their cloaks and flinging dust into the air, ²⁴the cohort commander ordered him to be brought into the compound and gave instruction that he be interrogated under the lash to determine the reason why they were making such an outcry against him. ²⁵But when they had stretched him out for the whips, Paul said to the centurion on duty, "Is it lawful for you to scourge a man who is a Roman citizen and has not been tried?" ²⁶When the centurion heard this, he went to the cohort commander and reported it, saying, "What are you going to do? This man is a Roman citi-

zen." ²⁷Then the commander came and said to him, "Tell me, are you a Roman citizen?" "Yes," he answered. ²⁸The commander replied, "I acquired this citizenship for a large sum of money." Paul said, "But I was born one." ²⁹At once those who were going to interrogate him backed away from him, and the commander became alarmed when he realized that he was a Roman citizen and that he had had him bound.

Paul before the Sanhedrin. ³⁰The next day, wishing to determine the truth about why he was being accused by the Jews, he freed him and ordered the chief priests and the whole Sanhedrin to convene. Then he brought Paul down and made him stand before them.

If Paul's adversaries are challenging his mission to Gentiles, the final part of the speech claims that the outreach to the nations was far from the action of an apostate. Like the great prophet Isaiah, Paul "saw the Lord" in the temple, protested his unworthiness, and received his mandate there, at the liturgical heart of Israel (v. 18; see Isa 6:1). In response, the crowd repeats the rejection of 21:36.

22:22-29 Paul imprisoned

Just as the tribune was caught in a false assumption about Paul earlier (that he was "the Egyptian," 21:38), now he is caught in another mistake about the Apostle's identity—assuming that this Jew is not a Roman citizen. Wrong again. This vivid drama, with Paul stretched out for interrogation under the lash and then rescued at the last minute, is more than good storytelling. It also demonstrates for Luke's readership that Paul, as a Roman citizen, is eminently qualified to mediate the gospel to the Roman world as well as to the Diaspora.

22:30–23:11 The investigation continues: Paul before the Sanhedrin

Having learned of Paul's Roman citizenship, the commander (Claudius Lysias, we learn in verse 26) tries a gentler mode of getting to the facts of the charges against Paul. He orders the chief priests and the

23 ¹Paul looked intently at the Sanhedrin and said, "My brothers, I have conducted myself with a perfectly clear conscience before God to this day." ²The high priest Ananias ordered his attendants to strike his mouth. ³Then Paul said to him, "God will strike you, you whitewashed wall. Do you indeed sit in judgment upon me according to the law and yet in violation of the law order me to be struck?" ⁴The attendants said, "Would you revile God's high priest?" ⁵Paul answered, "Brothers, I did not realize he was the high priest. For it is written, 'You shall not curse a ruler of your people.' "

⁶Paul was aware that some were Sadducees and some Pharisees, so he called out before the Sanhedrin, "My brothers, I am a Pharisee, the son of Pharisees; [I] am on trial for hope in the resurrection of the dead." ⁷When he said this, a dispute broke out between the Pharisees and Sadducees, and the group became divided. ⁸For the Sadducees say that there is no resurrection or angels or spirits, while the Pharisees acknowledge all three. ⁹A great uproar occurred, and some scribes belonging to the Pharisee party stood up and sharply argued, "We find nothing wrong with this man. Suppose a spirit or an angel has spoken to him?" ¹⁰The dispute was so serious that the commander, afraid that Paul would be torn to pieces by them, ordered his troops to go down and rescue him from their midst and take him into the compound.

---

full Sanhedrin to convene for a hearing. Notice that these people are not necessarily gathered as adversaries of Paul; they comprise the official Jewish body that the commander now looks to in order to discover whether Paul is a danger to Roman law and order. Thus we are not yet dealing with a trial; Lysias is still conducting a Roman investigation to see if Paul has done something that warrants a Roman trial.

Paul's declaration that he has always conducted himself with a clear conscience before God surely applies to his whole life and supports the notion that his experience on the road to Damascus is better understood as a prophetic call rather than a conversion, at least in the moral or religious sense.

The exchange between Paul and the high priest Ananias is loaded with irony. Paul comes across as a better exponent of the Law than does its official guardian. His assertion that he did not realize Ananias was the high priest implies that the latter's behavior, punishing an unconvicted person, was hardly the deportment expected of a person in that office.

Before any formal inquest begins, Paul asserts that he is a Pharisee (v. 6) and makes a simple proclamation of the gospel: "I am on trial for the hope in the resurrection of the dead." Commentators note Paul's shrewdness in playing the afterlife card, a key point of division between the two

[11]The following night the Lord stood by him and said, "Take courage. For just as you have borne witness to my cause in Jerusalem, so you must also bear witness in Rome."

Transfer to Caesarea. [12]When day came, the Jews made a plot and bound themselves by oath not to eat or drink until they had killed Paul. [13]There were more than forty who formed this conspiracy. [14]They went to the chief priests and elders and said, "We have bound ourselves by a solemn oath to taste nothing until we have killed Paul. [15]You, together with the Sanhedrin, must now make an official request to the commander to have him bring him down to you, as though you meant to investigate his case more thoroughly. We on our part are prepared to kill him before he arrives." [16]The son of Paul's sister, however, heard about the ambush; so he went and entered the compound and reported it to Paul. [17]Paul then called one of the centurions and requested, "Take this young man to the commander; he has something to report to him." [18]So he took him and brought him to the commander and explained, "The prisoner Paul called me and asked that I bring this young man to you; he has something to say to you." [19]The commander took him by the hand, drew him aside, and asked him pri-

---

parties. As Jesus' controversy with the Sadducees in Luke 20:27-40 demonstrated, Sadducees denied the resurrection. And as Luke notes here in a rare aside, neither did they believe in postmortem survival as "angel" or "spirit." For the Sadducees, if you could not find it in the Torah, it didn't count. This, of course, splits the Sanhedrin, with the Pharisees refusing to condemn Brother Paul.

But more is going on here than clever forensic strategy. By the time of Luke's writing of Acts, the high priest Ananias has indeed been "struck," assassinated in A.D. 66, according to Josephus. The Sadducees have ceased to exist as authorities, having lost their power base with the destruction of the temple by the Romans in A.D. 70. This leaves the Pharisees, the current leaders of formative Judaism, as the most important figures for Luke's readers. They emerge in this episode not so much as defenders of Paul but rather as men acting in bad will. Though they accept "the resurrection of the dead" as a hope, they resist Paul's testimony that the hoped-for resurrection has already begun concretely in Jesus of Nazareth.

It is this, rather than Paul's legal guilt or innocence, that will remain the issue for the remainder of the book. It is really the gospel that is on trial. In the context of the narrative, Paul's focus on the resurrection makes it clear to the Roman tribune (the most important auditor of this hearing) that the charges against Paul are Jewish matters, nothing of concern to imperial governance.

vately, "What is it you have to report to me?" [20]He replied, "The Jews have conspired to ask you to bring Paul down to the Sanhedrin tomorrow, as though they meant to inquire about him more thoroughly, [21]but do not believe them. More than forty of them are lying in wait for him; they have bound themselves by oath not to eat or drink until they have killed him. They are now ready and only wait for your consent." [22]As the commander dismissed the young man he directed him, "Tell no one that you gave me this information."

[23]Then he summoned two of the centurions and said, "Get two hundred soldiers ready to go to Caesarea by nine o'clock tonight, along with seventy horsemen and two hundred auxiliaries. [24]Provide mounts for Paul to ride and give him safe conduct to Felix the governor." [25]Then he wrote a letter with this content: [26]"Claudius Lysias to his excellency the governor Felix, greetings. [27]This man, seized by the Jews and about to be murdered by them, I rescued after intervening with my troops when I learned that he was a Roman citizen. [28]I wanted to learn the reason for their accusations against him so I brought him down to their Sanhedrin. [29]I discovered that he was accused in matters of controversial questions of their law and not of any charge deserving death or imprisonment. [30]Since it was brought to my attention that there will be a plot against the man, I am sending him to

23:12-35 A plot to assassinate Paul and a Roman rescue

A group of more than forty of Paul's co-religionists make a pact not to eat or drink until they have killed him. Luke offers no motive for such fanaticism. One can only surmise that these men exhibit the kind of rebellious zealotry that will come to expression some ten years later in the Zealot revolt against Rome in A.D. 67–70. They may have perceived in Paul's messianic mission to the Gentiles (and his rumored "watering down" of Jewish practices) a vitiation of Judean nationalism.

Tipped off by Paul's nephew regarding the plot to ambush his prisoner (v. 16), Lysias moves to place him in the protective custody of an armed cavalry, who are to escort him safely to the governor Felix (in office A.D. 52–59, the sixth prefect after Pontius Pilate).

Luke gives us the gist of the report Lysias sends to Felix. Given that our author has already provided his version of the events reported in the message, Luke no doubt expects the reader to smile at the way this Roman official tweaks the truth to put the best possible face on his conduct. We know from 21:27-40 that Lysias first quelled the riot, arrested Paul, and eventually ordered him interrogated under the lash. Only *then*, when Paul announced his citizenship, did the tribune first learn of it. As Lysias tells it in his report, his action with Paul was from the beginning a

you at once, and have also notified his accusers to state [their case] against him before you."

³¹So the soldiers, according to their orders, took Paul and escorted him by night to Antipatris. ³²The next day they returned to the compound, leaving the horsemen to complete the journey with him. ³³When they arrived in Caesarea they delivered the letter to the governor and presented Paul to him. ³⁴When he had read it and asked to what province he belonged, and learned that he was from Cilicia, ³⁵he said, "I shall hear your case when your accusers arrive." Then he ordered that he be held in custody in Herod's praetorium.

24 **Trial before Felix.** ¹Five days later the high priest Ananias came down with some elders and an advocate, a certain Tertullus, and they presented formal charges against Paul to the governor. ²When he was called, Tertullus began to accuse him, saying, "Since we have attained much peace through you, and reforms have been accomplished in this nation through your provident care, ³we acknowledge this in every way and everywhere, most excellent Felix, with all gratitude. ⁴But in order not to detain you further, I ask you to give us a brief hearing with your customary graciousness. ⁵We found this man to be a pest; he creates dissension among Jews all over the world and is a ringleader of the sect of the Nazoreans. ⁶He even tried to desecrate our temple, but we arrested him. [⁷] ⁸If you examine

---

bold rescue of a known Roman citizen. In his favor, his present "protective custody" action has in fact become such a rescue.

We may wonder why Felix, when he learns that Paul is from Cilicia, does not send him there for trial. In fact, Syria-Cilicia is a double province at this time (Vespasian will split it later), and Felix governs the area in which the charges have been brought against the accused. So he is responsible for the trial.

24:1-27 Paul is heard before Felix, in public and privately

Finally, with the arrival from Jerusalem of Ananias and some elders with their attorney, Paul faces a formal trial before the procurator Felix. After paying unctuous compliments to the governor, Tertullus, the prosecuting attorney, levels a set of broad and, as we readers know, unfounded charges against Paul: (a) he sows dissension among Jews all over the world [empire] (*oikoumenē*) and (b) he tried to profane the temple. Tertullus even tries to dignify with the term "arrest" (v. 6) what we know to have been an attempt at mob lynching.

As in his speech on the Antonia barracks steps to the crowd of would-be lynchers (Acts 22), Paul answers these false charges by rehearsing the facts that establish his exemplary and eminently traditional Jewish behavior. Far from desecrating the temple, he went there to worship their ancestral

him you will be able to learn from him for yourself about everything of which we are accusing him." ⁹The Jews also joined in the attack and asserted that these things were so.

¹⁰Then the governor motioned to him to speak and Paul replied, "I know that you have been a judge over this nation for many years and so I am pleased to make my defense before you. ¹¹As you can verify, not more than twelve days have passed since I went up to Jerusalem to worship. ¹²Neither in the temple, nor in the synagogues, nor anywhere in the city did they find me arguing with anyone or instigating a riot among the people. ¹³Nor can they prove to you the accusations they are now making against me. ¹⁴But this I do admit to you, that according to the Way, which they call a sect, I worship the God of our ancestors and I believe everything that is in accordance with the law and written in the prophets. ¹⁵I have the same hope in God as they themselves have that there will be a resurrection of the righteous and the unrighteous. ¹⁶Because of this, I always strive to keep my conscience clear before God and man. ¹⁷After many years, I came to bring alms for my nation and offerings. ¹⁸While I was so engaged, they found me, after my purification, in the temple without a crowd or disturbance. ¹⁹But some Jews from the province of Asia, who should be here

---

God. He is still a Torah-keeping Jew who worships the God he has always served in good conscience, except that now it is according to "the Way" that his adversaries dismiss as a "sect." Their charges are hearsay and therefore without merit. The original plaintiffs were the "Jews from . . . Asia" (21:27), but they are not present to testify. And the only thing that the present plaintiffs have witnessed was his proclamation that he is on trial "for the resurrection of the dead" (v. 21; see 23:6).

Paul's claim to have come "to bring alms for my nation and offerings" (v. 17) is the sole reference in Acts to his transmission of the Jerusalem relief fund (see Rom 15:25-26) as the main motive for his presence in Jerusalem. By calling the collection "alms for my nation" and linking it with his sponsoring of sacrifices for the nazirites fulfilling their vows, he casts those actions in language that associates them with the essence of Jewish piety. Felix's knowledge that Paul, as bearer of these funds, controls a substantial amount of money may well be what generated the governor's hope for a bribe (v. 26).

Since Felix is informed about "the Way" (through his Jewish wife Drusilla?), and since he has perhaps decided that the Way is no threat to Roman social order, he postpones judgment, pending further (unnecessary) consultation with Lysias. Felix allows two years to elapse without coming to judgment. Like most of the leaders in Luke-Acts, Jewish or

before you to make whatever accusation they might have against me—²⁰or let these men themselves state what crime they discovered when I stood before the Sanhedrin, ²¹unless it was my one outcry as I stood among them, that 'I am on trial before you today for the resurrection of the dead.' "

²²Then Felix, who was accurately informed about the Way, postponed the trial, saying, "When Lysias the commander comes down, I shall decide your case." ²³He gave orders to the centurion that he should be kept in custody but have some liberty, and that he should not prevent any of his friends from caring for his needs.

Captivity in Caesarea. ²⁴Several days later Felix came with his wife Drusilla, who was Jewish. He had Paul summoned and listened to him speak about faith in Christ Jesus. ²⁵But as he spoke about righteousness and self-restraint and the coming judgment, Felix became frightened and said, "You may go for now; when I find an opportunity I shall summon you again." ²⁶At the same time he hoped that a bribe would be offered him by Paul, and so he sent for him very often and conversed with him.

²⁷Two years passed and Felix was succeeded by Porcius Festus. Wishing to ingratiate himself with the Jews, Felix left Paul in prison.

25 **Appeal to Caesar.** ¹Three days after his arrival in the province, Festus went up from Caesarea to Jerusalem ²where the chief priests and Jew-

---

Roman, Felix wants chiefly to look after his own interests. (Regarding Felix's administration, the Roman historian Tacitus observes, "He exercised the power of a king with the spirit of the slave.")

25:1-12 Paul appeals to Caesar and comes before Agrippa

This chapter of Acts functions mainly as a transition. Luke is setting the scene for Paul's climactic speech before Agrippa in chapter 26. As he does so, he strengthens two themes important to his history: (a) the controversy regarding Paul and the Christian Way is a thoroughly Jewish matter, and (b) the legal structure and personnel of the Roman Empire are functioning at this time as instruments of divine Providence.

When Jewish leaders present their (now two-year-old) case against Paul and request that he be sent to them in Jerusalem (to be ambushed and killed along the way), Festus asserts his imperial authority. If they have charges to bring against a man in Roman custody, let them do it on the procurator's turf, before his tribunal in Caesarea (v. 5). Luke reflects Paul's adversaries' charges in Paul's response: he has done nothing against the Torah or against the temple *or against Caesar*. "Against Caesar" is a new note, paralleling the charges of the Sanhedrin against Jesus before Pilate (Luke 23:2). When Festus offers Paul the option of facing a formal trial

ish leaders presented him their formal charges against Paul. They asked him ³as a favor to have him sent to Jerusalem, for they were plotting to kill him along the way. ⁴Festus replied that Paul was being held in custody in Caesarea and that he himself would be returning there shortly. ⁵He said, "Let your authorities come down with me, and if this man has done something improper, let them accuse him."

⁶After spending no more than eight or ten days with them, he went down to Caesarea, and on the following day took his seat on the tribunal and ordered that Paul be brought in. ⁷When he appeared, the Jews who had come down from Jerusalem surrounded him and brought many serious charges against him, which they were unable to prove. ⁸In defending himself Paul said, "I have committed no crime either against the Jewish law or against the temple or against Caesar." ⁹Then Festus, wishing to ingratiate himself with the Jews, said to Paul in reply, "Are you willing to go up to Jerusalem and there stand trial before me on these charges?" ¹⁰Paul answered, "I am standing before the tribunal of Caesar; this is where I should be tried. I have committed no crime against the Jews, as you very well know. ¹¹If I have committed a crime or done anything deserving death, I do not seek to escape the death penalty; but if there is no substance to the charges they are bringing against me, then no one has the right to hand me over to them. I appeal to Caesar." ¹²Then Festus, after conferring with his council, replied, "You have appealed to Caesar. To Caesar you will go."

Paul before King Agrippa. ¹³When a few days had passed, King Agrippa

---

before the Sanhedrin in Jerusalem, he appeals to Caesar. This allows Festus to unburden himself of this case, and he decides to send Paul to Rome.

25:13-27 Paul before Agrippa

Enter King Agrippa and his twice-widowed sister Bernice. Agrippa—Herod Agrippa II—is the fourth Herod to appear in Luke's work. Herod the Great, the famous builder of Caesarea and Masada and spectacular renovator of the second temple, reigned at the time of the infancies of John the Baptist and Jesus (Luke 1:5). Herod the Tetrarch (Antipas), son of Herod the Great, ruled Galilee and Perea during the rest of Jesus' life. Herod Agrippa I (ruled A.D. 41–44), grandson of Herod the Great, appeared (and died) in Acts 12. Now we meet the great-grandson, Herod Agrippa II (who ruled after A.D. 50). We learn nothing new in Festus's report to Agrippa, but the way the report is expressed is telling. Festus characterizes the elders' charges as entirely a Jewish affair—"some issues . . . about their own religion"—much as Gallio spoke when he dismissed the Corinthian Jews' quarrel with Paul in Acts 18:15 and as Lysias wrote in his

and Bernice arrived in Caesarea on a visit to Festus. [14]Since they spent several days there, Festus referred Paul's case to the king, saying, "There is a man here left in custody by Felix. [15]When I was in Jerusalem the chief priests and the elders of the Jews brought charges against him and demanded his condemnation. [16]I answered them that it was not Roman practice to hand over an accused person before he has faced his accusers and had the opportunity to defend himself against their charge. [17]So when [they] came together here, I made no delay; the next day I took my seat on the tribunal and ordered the man to be brought in. [18]His accusers stood around him, but did not charge him with any of the crimes I suspected. [19]Instead they had some issues with him about their own religion and about a certain Jesus who had died but who Paul claimed was alive. [20]Since I was at a loss how to investigate this controversy, I asked if he were willing to go to Jerusalem and there stand trial on these charges. [21]And when Paul appealed that he be held in custody for the Emperor's decision, I ordered him held until I could send him to Caesar." [22]Agrippa said to Festus, "I too should like to hear this

report to Felix (23:29). There is a nice irony in the title used for the emperor in v. 26. The Greek word that our New American Bible version translates (accurately, in this context) as "our sovereign" is *ho kyrios* (literally, "the lord"). Given that the last instance of that word was a title for the risen Jesus (23:11) and the next instance, a few verses later, again refers to Jesus (26:15), the use of the title here (for Nero!) highlights the irony that the true lord of this history is not the emperor but Jesus—an irony that the book of Revelation will exploit richly.

When Festus invites Agrippa to interrogate Paul, it is not as a formal trial but rather as a hearing in the service of the Roman process; Festus hopes the Jewish king will come up with something substantive to report to Rome. This move also gives Luke the opportunity to underscore another parallel between the experience of the Apostle and his Master: as Procurator Pilate sent Jesus to the then current Jewish king (Herod Antipas) for a kind of hearing, so Procurator Festus presents Paul to another Jewish king. In Jesus' case, of course, Pilate was attempting to shunt the accused off to another jurisdiction. Festus, however, does not intend to let his charge slip out of Roman custody.

Verses 23-27 set the stage for Paul's final extended apologia in chapter 26. Luke packs the audience hall with an entourage that includes "cohort commanders and the prominent men of the city" (v. 23). Thus Paul will be addressing, along with Festus, Agrippa, and Bernice, powerful members of Caesarea's Gentile community.

man." He replied, "Tomorrow you will hear him."

²³The next day Agrippa and Bernice came with great ceremony and entered the audience hall in the company of cohort commanders and the prominent men of the city and, by command of Festus, Paul was brought in. ²⁴And Festus said, "King Agrippa and all you here present with us, look at this man about whom the whole Jewish populace petitioned me here and in Jerusalem, clamoring that he should live no longer. ²⁵I found, however, that he had done nothing deserving death, and so when he appealed to the Emperor, I decided to send him. ²⁶But I have nothing definite to write about him to our sovereign; therefore I have brought him before all of you, and particularly before you, King Agrippa, so that I may have something to write as a result of this investigation. ²⁷For it seems senseless to me to send up a prisoner without indicating the charges against him."

26 **King Agrippa Hears Paul.** ¹Then Agrippa said to Paul, "You may now speak on your own behalf." So Paul stretched out his hand and began his defense. ²"I count myself fortunate, King Agrippa, that I am to defend myself before you today against all the charges made against me by the Jews, ³especially since you are an expert in all the Jewish customs and controversies. And therefore I beg you to listen patiently. ⁴My manner of living

26:1-23 The inquest before Governor Festus and King Agrippa

The speech that Paul gives to these powerful representatives of the Jewish and Gentile communities is, like the speeches in Acts 2, 3, 13, and 17, one of Luke's theological masterpieces. Much of what we denote by the post-biblical terms "ecclesiology" (theology of church), "Christology" (how Jesus is the Messiah), and "soteriology" (theory of salvation) Luke communicates through this speech.

First, Luke highlights Paul speaking as an expert Jew (a Pharisee, and therefore one highly trained in Israelite tradition) to a well-informed Jewish leader (Agrippa was completing the project of his great-grandfather, the renovation of the Second Temple). Moreover, Paul had demonstrated his zeal for his people's tradition in his efforts against what he had at first perceived as a threat to those traditions, the Way of the Jesus people. To top it off, the centerpiece of his teaching and preaching is the essence of Jewish hope—resurrection from the dead. The unmentioned novelty, of course, is that Paul and the rest of the people of the Way have been announcing that the expected end-time general resurrection has been stunningly anticipated by the resurrection of a single person, Jesus of Nazareth (see the reference to "the first to rise from the dead" at verse 23).

from my youth, a life spent from the beginning among my people and in Jerusalem, all [the] Jews know. ⁵They have known about me from the start, if they are willing to testify, that I have lived my life as a Pharisee, the strictest party of our religion. ⁶But now I am standing trial because of my hope in the promise made by God to our ancestors. ⁷Our twelve tribes hope to attain to that promise as they fervently worship God day and night; and on account of this hope I am accused by Jews, O king. ⁸Why is it thought unbelievable among you that God raises the dead? ⁹I myself once thought that I had to do many things against the name of Jesus the Nazorean, ¹⁰and I did so in Jerusalem. I imprisoned many of the holy ones with the authorization I received from the chief priests, and when they were to be put to death I cast my vote against them. ¹¹Many times, in synagogue after synagogue, I punished them in an attempt to force them to blaspheme; I was so enraged against them that I pursued them even to foreign cities.

¹²"On one such occasion I was traveling to Damascus with the authorization and commission of the chief priests. ¹³At midday, along the way, O king, I saw a light from the sky,

---

Paul then recounts for the second time the experience on the road to Damascus, making it the third time for us readers (who first heard of it in the original narrative of Acts 9 and then in the speech of Acts 22). The variations in the details and language in this third telling are far more than an effort at literary variety. The language about light, darkness, and seeing participates in a consistent symbolic theme carrying powerful implications.

This time the light from the sky *is brighter than the noonday sun*, flattening *everyone* to the ground. And the language about blindness—which was quite literally physical in the Acts 9 account, then muted in the Acts 22 version—is not even applied to Paul here. That imagery now describes the experience of Gentile converts. Here the emphasis is on the fact that Paul will witness to what he *has seen* and that he is being missioned to *open the eyes of the Gentiles* so that *they may turn from darkness to light*. Thus what Paul first experienced literally in his physical blindness in the first account becomes a metaphor for the Christian mission to the nations in this third account. This metaphor is developed further at the climax of the speech: Paul is saying "nothing different from what the prophets and Moses foretold, that the Messiah must suffer and that, as the first to rise from the dead, he would *proclaim light both to our people and to the Gentiles*" (vv. 22-23, emphasis added).

And how, precisely, does Luke understand that the risen Messiah "proclaims light" after the resurrection? The whole of Luke-Acts answers that

brighter than the sun, shining around me and my traveling companions. [14]We all fell to the ground and I heard a voice saying to me in Hebrew, 'Saul, Saul, why are you persecuting me? It is hard for you to kick against the goad.' [15]And I said, 'Who are you, sir?' And the Lord replied, 'I am Jesus whom you are persecuting. [16]Get up now, and stand on your feet. I have appeared to you for this purpose, to appoint you as a servant and witness of what you have seen [of me] and what you will be shown. [17]I shall deliver you from this people and from the Gentiles to whom I send you, [18]to open their eyes that they may turn from darkness to light and from the power of Satan to God, so that they may obtain forgiveness of sins and an inheritance among those who have been consecrated by faith in me.'

[19]"And so, King Agrippa, I was not disobedient to the heavenly vision. [20]On the contrary, first to those in Damascus and in Jerusalem and throughout the whole country of Judea, and then to the Gentiles, I preached the need to repent and turn to God, and to do works

---

question, especially in its use of quotations of Isaiah. At Luke 2:30-32, during the presentation in the temple, when Simeon takes the child Jesus into his arms and sings his famous *Nunc Dimittis,* he draws upon Isaiah's imagery of vision and light: "for my eyes have seen your salvation [LXX Isa 40:5] / which you prepared in sight of all the peoples, / a light for revelation to the Gentiles [Isa 42:6; 49:6], / and glory for your people Israel."

At his debut in Nazareth, Jesus employs LXX Isaiah 61:1-2 to characterize his mission, and the center of that quotation is "He has sent me to proclaim . . . recovery of sight to the blind" (Luke 4:18). Jesus does indeed give sight to the blind in the physical cure of the blind in his pre-Easter activity (Luke 7:21; 18:35-43), but it takes the post-Easter activity of the church in Acts to fulfill the promise of the Servant functioning as a light to the Gentiles. Luke makes that quite explicit when, at the synagogue in Pisidian Antioch, he has Paul and Barnabas (both!) say, "We now turn to the Gentiles. For so the Lord has commanded us, 'I have made you a light to the Gentiles, that you may be an instrument of salvation to the ends of the earth'" (Acts 13:46-47; see Isa 49:6). Strikingly, language describing the Servant of Yahweh in Isaiah, earlier applied to Jesus by Simeon, is now applied to the post-Easter continuation of Jesus' mission by his followers. Thus when we hear the reference to the risen Christ proclaiming "light to the Gentiles" at the climax of Paul's speech in Acts 26, we know that what Paul and the rest of the church are doing is not only in continuity with Jesus' mission but their work is somehow the work of the risen Lord himself.

This was the import of Paul's vision on the road to Damascus ("Saul, Saul, why are you persecuting me?"—v. 14b). The risen Lord is identified

giving evidence of repentance. ²¹That is why the Jews seized me [when I was] in the temple and tried to kill me. ²²But I have enjoyed God's help to this very day, and so I stand here testifying to small and great alike, saying nothing different from what the prophets and Moses foretold, ²³that the Messiah must suffer and that, as the first to rise from the dead, he would proclaim light both to our people and to the Gentiles."

Reactions to Paul's Speech. ²⁴While Paul was so speaking in his defense, Festus said in a loud voice, "You are mad, Paul; much learning is driving you mad." ²⁵But Paul replied, "I am not mad, most excellent Festus; I am speaking words of truth and reason. ²⁶The king knows about these matters and to him I speak boldly, for I cannot believe that [any] of this has escaped his notice; this was not done in a corner. ²⁷King Agrippa, do you believe the prophets? I know you believe." ²⁸Then Agrippa said to Paul, "You will soon persuade me to play the Christian." ²⁹Paul replied, "I would pray to God that sooner or later not only you but all who listen to me today might become as I am except for these chains."

³⁰Then the king rose, and with him the governor and Bernice and the others who sat with them. ³¹And after they had withdrawn they said to one an-

---

with the believing community, and through them he opens the eyes of the nations and brings them from darkness to light. At the end of the book, Luke will have Paul use Isaiah 6:9-10 ("They have closed their eyes, / so that they may not see with their eyes") to characterize those of Israel who, like Saul before his conversion, fail to respond to the mission.

Whereas Festus responds to the defense simply with amazement ("You are mad, Paul") and Agrippa with cynicism, Festus, Bernice, and the rest comment that Paul is doing nothing that deserves death or imprisonment (v. 31). Thus, like Jesus (see Luke 23:4, 14, and 22), Paul is declared innocent three times by Roman officials and a Jewish king (Lysias, 23:29; Festus, 25:25; and Agrippa, 26:31-32). And also like (and with) Jesus, he is fulfilling Servant Israel's vocation to be a light to the nations.

27:1-44 To Rome: storm, shipwreck, and survival

As he nears the end of his history, Luke gives us a whopping good sea adventure. Some recent commentators have wondered why Luke, who can be so sparse in his treatment of such momentous events as, for example, the early spread of the Christian mission into the Hellenistic world (11:20-21), decides at this point to spend so much parchment on the details of Paul's voyage to Rome. Some scholars, subscribing to the theory that the "we" sections are a literary convention and noting resonances with other ancient accounts of shipwreck, have suggested that Luke has imaginatively

other, "This man is doing nothing [at all] that deserves death or imprisonment." [32]And Agrippa said to Festus, "This man could have been set free if he had not appealed to Caesar."

27 Departure for Rome. [1]When it was decided that we should sail to Italy, they handed Paul and some other prisoners over to a centurion named Julius of the Cohort Augusta. [2]We went on board a ship from Adramyttium bound for ports in the province of Asia and set sail. Aristarchus, a Macedonian from Thessalonica, was with us. [3]On the following day we put in at Sidon where Julius was kind enough to allow Paul to visit his friends who took care of him. [4]From there we put out to sea and sailed around the sheltered side of Cyprus because of the headwinds, [5]and crossing the open sea off the coast of Cilicia and Pamphylia we came to Myra in Lycia.

Storm and Shipwreck. [6]There the centurion found an Alexandrian ship that was sailing to Italy and put us on board. [7]For many days we made little headway, arriving at Cnidus only with difficulty, and because the wind would not permit us to continue our course

embellished some minimal facts available to him regarding Paul's voyage. Others, noting the abundance of nautical technical terms, posit that Luke took over an available voyage account and applied it to Paul.

It is, however, simpler and more reasonable to presume that Luke is sparse when his sources are sparse and that he willingly shares details when he has access to them, especially when he was an eyewitness to the events he describes. The first-person plural of this final "we" section (27:1–28:16) supports such an interpretation. Moreover, we have no evidence of the "we" form used as a literary convention in ancient history writing by authors who are not describing their own experience.

That Paul himself was richly experienced in sea travel and its dangers is clear from his remark in 2 Corinthians 11:25: "Three times I was shipwrecked, I passed a night and a day on the deep . . . ." And the tradition that Luke was a close companion of Paul is firm (Phlm 24; Col 4:14; and 2 Tim 4:11). There is no reason to presume that he was inexperienced in sea travel or lacked the vocabulary to describe it. Of course, master storyteller that he is, he knows he has a "good yarn" here. He tells it with relish and in a way that serves his history of what God has accomplished in and through these events, which could be called the passion and vindication of the Apostle Paul.

As a Roman citizen, Paul, accompanied by his faithful companion Aristarchus (see 19:29; 20:4; Col 4:10; and Phlm 24) and the narrator (presumably Luke), is placed under the protective custody of a centurion, one

we sailed for the sheltered side of Crete off Salmone. ⁸We sailed past it with difficulty and reached a place called Fair Havens, near which was the city of Lasea.

⁹Much time had now passed and sailing had become hazardous because the time of the fast had already gone by, so Paul warned them, ¹⁰"Men, I can see that this voyage will result in severe damage and heavy loss not only to the cargo and the ship, but also to our lives." ¹¹The centurion, however, paid more attention to the pilot and to the owner of the ship than to what Paul said. ¹²Since the harbor was unfavorably situated for spending the winter,

the majority planned to put out to sea from there in the hope of reaching Phoenix, a port in Crete facing west-northwest, there to spend the winter.

¹³A south wind blew gently, and thinking they had attained their objective, they weighed anchor and sailed along close to the coast of Crete. ¹⁴Before long an offshore wind of hurricane force called a "Northeaster" struck. ¹⁵Since the ship was caught up in it and could not head into the wind we gave way and let ourselves be driven. ¹⁶We passed along the sheltered side of an island named Cauda and managed only with difficulty to get the dinghy under control. ¹⁷They hoisted it aboard, then

---

Julius. There being no commercial passenger ships in antiquity, Julius books passage on a ship returning to the Aegean area. The "philanthropic" (*philanthropos*) Julius allows Paul to visit friends, probably Christians, during a stop at Sidon. Because of the late fall weather, the ship hugs the coast, passing behind the shelter of Cyprus. At Myra they transfer to an Alexandrian grain ship headed for Italy. When they put in at Fair Havens, in the mid-south side of the island of Crete, Paul advises wintering there, since continuing now would entail loss of cargo and lives—reasonable advice that will turn out, in the end, to be only partly accurate.

When the voyage continues and a hurricane wind (a "northeaster") forces them dangerously off course, Paul provides quite a different sort of message. A dream vision enables him to urge courage and to predict (more accurately than his earlier commonsense prediction) safety to all aboard. The God he belongs to and serves would save them. It is significant that he says "God" rather than "the Lord Jesus" here; it is language that a pagan audience would more easily understand, and Luke is emphasizing that it is the maker of heaven and earth who is managing what is going forward in the midst of this chaos of nature.

Speaking of Luke's use of language, one cannot help noting that the description of Paul, acting in the manner of the host presiding at a Jewish meal (taking bread, thanking God, breaking the bread), evokes the

used cables to undergird the ship. Because of their fear that they would run aground on the shoal of Syrtis, they lowered the drift anchor and were carried along in this way. ¹⁸We were being pounded by the storm so violently that the next day they jettisoned some cargo, ¹⁹and on the third day with their own hands they threw even the ship's tackle overboard. ²⁰Neither the sun nor the stars were visible for many days, and no small storm raged. Finally, all hope of our surviving was taken away.

²¹When many would no longer eat, Paul stood among them and said, "Men, you should have taken my advice and not have set sail from Crete and you would have avoided this disastrous loss. ²²I urge you now to keep up your courage; not one of you will be lost, only the ship. ²³For last night an angel of the God to whom [I] belong and whom I serve stood by me ²⁴and said, 'Do not be afraid, Paul. You are destined to stand before Caesar; and behold, for your sake, God has granted safety to all who are sailing with you.' ²⁵Therefore, keep up your courage, men; I trust in God that it will turn out as I have been told. ²⁶We are destined to run aground on some island."

²⁷On the fourteenth night, as we were still being driven about on the Adriatic Sea, toward midnight the sailors began to suspect that they were nearing land. ²⁸They took soundings

---

language of the Last Supper and Christian Eucharist. Most commentators rightly insist that Luke surely does *not* mean to say that Paul, attended by his two Christian companions, is presiding at a Christian celebration of the Lord's Supper before a "congregation" of 273 pagans! At the same time, Luke the savvy wordsmith surely knows that his Christian readers (or hearers) would catch the resonance with the Christian liturgy (and with Luke 5:16 and 22:19).

Indeed, once that resonance is heard in verse 35, further resonances abound. For example:

1) Immediately before this mealtime blessing, Paul had said, "Not a hair of the head of anyone of you will be lost." This, of course, repeats what Jesus had said in his end-time discourse (Luke 21:18), which also speaks of "signs in the *sun,* the moon, *and the stars,*" and asserts that "on earth nations will be in dismay, *perplexed by the roaring of the sea and the waves*" (Luke 21:25, emphasis added). In this literal experience of such a sea, Luke has made a point of noting that "neither the sun nor the stars were visible for many days" (Acts 27:20).

2) In a way that is more obvious in Greek than in English translation, Luke uses "salvation" language suggestively. The words used to describe physical survival of storm and shipwreck in this account (*sōzō* in vv. 20, 31; *sōtēria* in v. 34) are, to be sure, the usual words for describing rescue

and found twenty fathoms; a little farther on, they again took soundings and found fifteen fathoms. ²⁹Fearing that we would run aground on a rocky coast, they dropped four anchors from the stern and prayed for day to come. ³⁰The sailors then tried to abandon ship; they lowered the dinghy to the sea on the pretext of going to lay out anchors from the bow. ³¹But Paul said to the centurion and the soldiers, "Unless these men stay with the ship, you cannot be saved." ³²So the soldiers cut the ropes of the dinghy and set it adrift.

³³Until the day began to dawn, Paul kept urging all to take some food. He said, "Today is the fourteenth day that you have been waiting, going hungry and eating nothing. ³⁴I urge you, therefore, to take some food; it will help you survive. Not a hair of the head of anyone of you will be lost." ³⁵When he said this, he took bread, gave thanks to God in front of them all, broke it, and began to eat. ³⁶They were all encouraged, and took some food themselves. ³⁷In all, there were two hundred seventy-six of us on the ship. ³⁸After they had eaten enough, they lightened the ship by throwing the wheat into the sea.

³⁹When day came they did not recognize the land, but made out a bay with a beach. They planned to run the ship ashore on it, if they could. ⁴⁰So they cast off the anchors and abandoned them to the sea, and at the same

---

and survival; but in Luke's work, they are also used for salvation in the ultimate (eschatological) sense (e.g., *sōtēria*, "salvation," at Luke 1:77 [forgiveness of sins]; at 19:9 [Zacchaeus's conversion]; and at Acts 4:12; 13:26, 47; *sōtērion*, "salvation," at Luke 2:20 and 3:6 [Isa 40:5]; *sōzō*, the verbal form of "save," at Luke 7:50; 8:12; 13:23; 17:19; 18:26; 19:10; Acts 2:21 [Joel 3:5]; 2:47; 4:12; and 15:1, 11). That diction makes it easy, even inevitable, that readers will hear salvation overtones in the storm and shipwreck account of Acts 27.

3) Finally, in an extended work that has thematized the importance of detachment from material goods on the Christian journey of following Jesus, all the literally realistic details of dumping cargo, jettisoning gear, cutting off the dinghy, and abandoning anchors point to the need for traveling light to achieve salvation. (See Luke 10:4; 14:33; 18:25-27: "'For it is easier for a camel to pass through the eye of a needle than for a rich person to enter the kingdom of God.' Those who heard this said, 'Then who can be saved?' And he said, 'What is impossible for human beings is possible for God.'")

This is not to say that Luke has composed an allegory of Christian life in Acts 27. Rather, he has reported this tale of God's care of Paul and his mission in such a way that the historical account of nautical disaster and

time they unfastened the lines of the rudders, and hoisting the foresail into the wind, they made for the beach. [41]But they struck a sandbar and ran the ship aground. The bow was wedged in and could not be moved, but the stern began to break up under the pounding [of the waves]. [42]The soldiers planned to kill the prisoners so that none might swim away and escape, [43]but the centurion wanted to save Paul and so kept them from carrying out their plan. He ordered those who could swim to jump overboard first and get to the shore, [44]and then the rest, some on planks, others on debris from the ship. In this way, all reached shore safely.

28 **Winter in Malta.** [1]Once we had reached safety we learned that the island was called Malta. [2]The natives showed us extraordinary hospitality; they lit a fire and welcomed all of us because it had begun to rain and was cold. [3]Paul had gathered a bundle of brushwood and was putting it on the fire when a viper, escaping from the heat, fastened on his hand. [4]When the natives saw the snake hanging from his hand, they said to one another, "This man must certainly be a murderer; though he escaped the sea, Justice has not let him remain alive." [5]But he shook the snake off into the fire and suffered no harm. [6]They were expecting him to

---

survival resonates with and alludes to the end-time situation of the church and the world. (We are "all in the same boat," and God is our only hope.) A further clue that Luke has this resonance in mind may be the fact that only his version of the synoptic tradition of the stilling of the storm pictures Jesus and the disciples as *sailing* (*pleontōn*, Luke 8:23).

28:1-10 Malta: hospitality, vindication, and healing

The story of the sea travel, including the "we" section that tells it, continues through the arrival in Rome (in verse 16, where the New American Bible translates "he entered," the Greek has "*we* entered"). The safe arrival of all 276 on the shore of Malta leads to a supreme irony. Everything has been building, we readers have been led to believe, to a trial and judgment by the highest authority of the secular world, Caesar. But Luke will end his second volume without any mention of that Roman trial (which, tradition tells us, resulted in Paul's death). Instead, we are told of judgment by a lower, more spontaneous "court," reflecting the higher, divine judgment.

In Mediterranean antiquity, survival of disaster demonstrated divine favor. Luke calls the hospitable Maltese natives *barbaroi* (that is, non-Greek-speakers), but he speaks of their uncommon *philanthropia*. When they see Paul attacked by a snake, they interpret that as a sign of divine disfavor—indeed, proof that Paul is a murderer (v. 5). However, when he

swell up or suddenly to fall down dead but, after waiting a long time and seeing nothing unusual happen to him, they changed their minds and began to say that he was a god. [7]In the vicinity of that place were lands belonging to a man named Publius, the chief of the island. He welcomed us and received us cordially as his guests for three days. [8]It so happened that the father of Publius was sick with a fever and dysentery. Paul visited him and, after praying, laid his hands on him and healed him. [9]After this had taken place, the rest of the sick on the island came to Paul and were cured. [10]They paid us great honor and when we eventually set sail they brought us the provisions we needed.

Arrival in Rome. [11]Three months later we set sail on a ship that had wintered at the island. It was an Alexandrian ship with the Dioscuri as its figurehead. [12]We put in at Syracuse and stayed there three days, [13]and from there we sailed round the coast and arrived at Rhegium. After a day, a south wind came up and in two days we reached Puteoli. [14]There we found some brothers and were urged to stay with them for seven days. And thus we

---

fails to swell up and drop dead, they call him a god! An overreaction, to be sure, but a powerful point has been made. As God had vindicated Jesus through resurrection, so he vindicates Paul through rescue from storm and snakebite. Further affirmation comes by way of Paul's ability to extend Jesus' healing ministry to the father of Governor Publius and other sick of the island who come to him.

28:11-31 Arrival in Rome and testimony to Jews

How a work ends is a matter of great importance to any careful author, especially in antiquity (recall Aristotle's stress on the importance of a beginning, middle, and end of a work). Luke chooses to end his two-volume work, not, as we already observed, with the expected Roman trial, but with several encounters between Paul and local Jewish leaders. Because these dialogues issue in "mixed reviews" at best and end with Paul quoting Isaiah 6:9-10 and turning once again to Gentiles, some commentators have read this as a declaration that God has, at this point, severed his covenant relationship with the Jews. Since this kind of interpretation has supported Christian anti-Judaism, it is important to read Luke's narrative ending carefully, on its own terms.

The first contact that Paul and his two companions make on Italian soil is with people in Puteoli, whom Luke calls "brothers." Since it is the Gentile Luke who refers to them as brothers, the presumption is that they are fellow Christians. After a week of enjoying their hospitality (the Roman guard himself apparently glad for the break), they move on to the Forum

came to Rome. [15]The brothers from there heard about us and came as far as the Forum of Appius and Three Taverns to meet us. On seeing them, Paul gave thanks to God and took courage. [16]When he entered Rome, Paul was allowed to live by himself, with the soldier who was guarding him.

Testimony to Jews in Rome. [17]Three days later he called together the leaders of the Jews. When they had gathered he said to them, "My brothers, although I had done nothing against our people or our ancestral customs, I was handed over to the Romans as a prisoner from Jerusalem. [18]After trying my case the Romans wanted to release me, because they found nothing against me deserving the death penalty. [19]But when the Jews objected, I was obliged to appeal to Caesar, even though I had no accusation to make against my own nation. [20]This is the reason, then, I have requested to see you and to speak with you, for it is on account of the hope of Israel that I wear these chains." [21]They answered him, "We have received no letters from Judea about you, nor has any of the brothers arrived with a damaging report or rumor about you. [22]But we should like to hear you present your views, for we know that this sect is denounced everywhere."

[23]So they arranged a day with him and came to his lodgings in great numbers. From early morning until evening,

of Appius and then to the rest stop called Three Taverns. At both places brothers come down from Rome to meet them. Paul's response to the brothers ("Paul gave thanks to God and took courage," v. 15) confirms the likelihood that these are also Christians. (The Christian community in Rome had been founded by others than Paul or Peter, possibly by the "travelers from Rome" [2:10] who had witnessed the birth of the church at Pentecost.)

The author James D. G. Dunn makes a charming interpretive conjecture regarding Luke's inclusion of the name of the Alexandrian ship that takes Paul's party to Rome, the *Dioscuri* ("Zeus's Boys," that is, Castor and Pollux, twin sons of the god Zeus). Noting that Luke uses "brothers" four times in the next few verses, first of Christians then of Jews, this author suggests that Luke calls attention to the name of the ship because for him the Christian and Jewish "brothers" that Paul is about to encounter are "indeed twin children of the one God, brothers of Paul, and so of one another."

Once established in Rome, apparently under house arrest in his own rented lodgings (v. 28), Paul calls together (non-Christian) Jewish leaders, who are also called "brothers" (vv. 17 and 21). His purpose is a kind of preemptive defense. Since the plaintiffs in his case are the Jerusalem Jews, he presents his apologia to their Roman counterparts. For us readers, the

The Temple of the Castors and the Arch of Titus on the Roman Forum

he expounded his position to them, bearing witness to the kingdom of God and trying to convince them about Jesus from the law of Moses and the prophets. 24Some were convinced by what he had said, while others did not believe. 25Without reaching any agreement among themselves they began to leave; then Paul made one final statement. "Well did the holy Spirit speak to your ancestors through the prophet Isaiah, saying:
26'Go to this people and say:

You shall indeed hear but not understand.
You shall indeed look but never see.
27Gross is the heart of this people;
they will not hear with their ears;
they have closed their eyes,
so they may not see with their eyes
and hear with their ears
and understand with their heart
and be converted,
and I heal them.'

---

defense is familiar: the Roman authorities in Caesarea have not found him guilty of anything warranting the death penalty, and his behavior is perfectly Jewish: he preaches "the hope of Israel." What is new is his hinting at the possibility (not pursued) of a countersuit (v. 19). They reply that they have heard nothing bad about him, by letter or hearsay. But they have heard about this controversial "sect" that he promotes, and they do want to learn more about that.

To this end, Paul holds an all-day conference with an even greater number of Jewish leaders, focusing on the heart of the matter: the kingdom of God and Jesus as fulfillment of the Scriptures. Some are convinced, others are not, and they leave without agreeing among themselves. As commentary on this divided response, Paul invokes Isaiah 6:9-10, implying that those who have failed to accept Jesus as the hope of Israel have fulfilled that prophecy. He adds, alluding to LXX Isa 40:5 (quoted earlier at Luke 3:6), that "this salvation of God has been sent to the Gentiles; they will listen."

Does this final word of Paul mean that the door is closed to further mission to Israel? No more than the presence of Isaiah 6:9-10 in the original commission of Isaiah of Jerusalem indicated that he had no mission to his people (belied by the sixty chapters that follow in the scroll of Isaiah). The rejection of the gospel by the majority of historical Israel is, for Luke, a fact to be faced. But this fact, and the turn to the Gentiles, is no more a definitive dismissal of the Jews than are the parallel moments in the synagogues of Pisidian Antioch (13:46-47) or Corinth (18:6). In ending with this episode, Luke has helped his (largely Gentile) readers understand (a) their relationship to historical Israel, (b) the majority of Israel's rejection of

²⁸Let it be known to you that this salvation of God has been sent to the Gentiles; they will listen." [²⁹]

³⁰He remained for two full years in his lodgings. He received all who came to him, ³¹and with complete assurance and without hindrance he proclaimed the kingdom of God and taught about the Lord Jesus Christ.

---

its Messiah, and (c) how the Gentiles have become beneficiaries of Israel's vocation to be a "light to the nations" (Isa 49:6).

Meanwhile, in the spirit of the parables of the barren fig tree (Luke 13:6-9) and two lost sons (Luke 15:11-32), the door remains open. In Paul's continued ministry during his house arrest, he receives "*all* who came to him" (emphasis added). He models the community's ongoing mission as "he proclaimed the kingdom of God and taught about the Lord Jesus Christ with boldness of speech [*meta parrēsias*], without hindrance [*akōlytōs*]" (v. 31, my translation). Note that the last two words powerfully affirm the theme of freedom running through the whole of Acts; *parrēsia* is that same freedom and boldness of speech for which the community prayed in Acts 4:29 and which the leaders exhibit throughout Acts (2:29; 4:13, 31; 9:27-28; 13:46; 14:3; 18:26; 19:8; and 26:25). And the final word, *akōlytōs* ("without hindrance") reminds us that neither the one who was sent to proclaim release to prisoners (Luke 4:18) nor his Spirit-led followers were hindered by imprisonment or even death.

Luke's two-volume work, which began in the Jerusalem temple, ends with the mission continuing unabated in a rented Roman apartment. In the end, Luke's history is not so much about Peter or Paul as about the fidelity of God and the continuing prophetic mission of the followers of Jesus. If the ending of Acts surprises us by failing to include the martyrdom of Paul (which was surely known to Luke), that very inconclusiveness serves to remind us that we are invited to continue the story with our lives.

REVIEW AIDS AND DISCUSSION TOPICS

Introduction *(pages 5–10)*

1. Why is it important to read the Acts of the Apostles as a sequel to the Gospel of Luke?

2. What are the pros and cons of the present arrangement of printed Bibles (Luke, then John, then Acts)?

3. Why are the speeches in Acts more valuable than transcriptions ("tapes") of what Peter, Stephen, and Paul said?

4. What does Luke 1:1-4 tell the reader about Luke's purposes in writing Luke-Acts?

5. What are some clues to the unity of Luke-Acts?

1:1–8:3 The risen Christ and the restoration of Israel in Jerusalem *(pages 11–41)*

1. How does Acts 1:8, in conjunction with Isaiah 49:5-6, provide a kind of table of contents for Acts?

2. What is the biblical background for the phrase "baptized in the holy Spirit" (1:5)?

3. Why is the restoration of "the Twelve" so important to Luke?

4. How does knowledge about the Feast of Weeks help us understand the Christian experience of Pentecost (Acts 2)?

5. How does Peter's quotation of Joel and Psalm 16 help him proclaim the Pentecost experiences as signs of the resurrection of Jesus and the presence of the end times?

6. How does Luke's description of the Jerusalem Christian community (2:42-47) tell us about what the church is meant to be always? Is this a romantic ideal or something that you have met in experience?

7. Why does Luke highlight the healing of the man born lame (Acts 3)?

8. How does the leaping in Isaiah 35:5-6 help us understand the Gospel meaning of this healing?

9. The applications of Psalms 2 and 118 to celebrate Christian events and experience (Acts 4): Are these applications simply arbitrary? Or do they truly fulfill the meaning of the Hebrew psalms?

10. What was sinful about the actions of Ananias and Sapphira (Acts 5)?

11. What does the narrative about the selection of the Seven (Acts 6) suggest about the church's ability to adapt in order to deal with crises?

12. In Stephen's speech (Acts 7), what do the stories of Joseph and Moses have to do with Jesus?

13. How does Acts 7 address the question? What makes for true worship of God?

8:4–9:43 The mission in Judea and Samaria *(pages 42–49)*

1. How does the conversion of the Ethiopian eunuch fulfill Scripture (Acts 8:26-40)?

2. How does this inclusion of an outcast apply today?

3. Saul's (Paul's) experience on the road to Damascus (Acts 9)—is it best called a conversion, a commissioning, or both?

4. How does Saul's (Paul's) experience show up in some of his epistles?

10:1–15:35 The inauguration of the Gentile mission *(pages 49–74)*

1. What does Peter's vision of the animals in the sheet have to do with his encounter with the household of Cornelius (Acts 10)?

2. Why is the conversion of Cornelius so important for Luke's account of the early church?

3. What further light does Peter's speech in chapter 11 throw on the meaning of his encounter with Cornelius's household?

4. In his final words to the congregation in the synagogue of Pisidian Antioch, what fresh application does Paul give to the quotation from Isaiah: "I have made you a light to the Gentiles, that you may be an instrument of salvation to the end of the earth" (Acts 13:47)?

5. What is Luke's point in emphasizing the parallels between the healing of the man born lame by Peter and John in Acts 3 and the healing of the man born lame by Paul and Barnabas in Acts 14?

6. Regarding the Jerusalem Council (Acts 15), what was the crisis that occasioned this leadership meeting? How did Luke's account of that meeting provide a model for decision-making in the church?

15:36–28:31 The mission of Paul to the ends of the earth *(pages 74–125)*

The Aegean Mission: Journeys two and three—Acts 16–21

1. Why do you think Luke highlights Lydia (ch. 16)?

2. What did Paul and Silas find objectionable in the unsolicited advertising of the possessed girl?

3. Paul's famous speech in Athens (ch. 17)—do you think it was a flop? Or is it rather a model of interreligious dialogue even today?

4. What is the significance of each of these figures, mentioned in Luke's account of the Corinthian ministry (Acts 18): Aquilia, Priscilla, Apollos, Gallio?

5. What does Paul's farewell address to the Ephesian elders (Acts 20) have in common with Jesus' farewell address to the disciples at the Last Supper (Luke 22:25-38)?

6. How do you reconcile Paul's attitude about the Law in, say, the letter to the Romans ("a person is justified by faith apart from works of the law," Rom 3:28) and his readiness to sponsor sacrifices in the temple (Acts 21:15-26)?

To Rome: Paul defends himself and the Word—Acts 22–28

1. In Paul's first defense speech (Acts 22), he recounts the story of his conversion and commissioning that the reader has already heard in chapter 9; what is the point of the repetition and the variations and additions in this version of his experience?

2. What is the effect of Paul's strategy when he faces the Sanhedrin (Acts 23)? How does this relate to Luke's larger purpose?

3. What does Paul's speech before the procurator Felix (Acts 24) reveal about Paul? And what does the passage reveal about Felix?

4. In Paul's speech before Festus and Agrippa (Acts 26), how does Isaiah's description of Servant Israel ("a light for the nation," Isa 49:6) apply both to Jesus and to Paul, and implicitly the church? How does the imagery about blindness and seeing change in the

three accounts of Paul's conversion/commission in Acts 9, 22, and 26?

5. In Luke's narrative of voyage, shipwreck, and survival (Acts 27), what details suggest that Luke has more than entertainment as his purpose for devoting so much parchment to it?

6. Some commentators have interpreted Luke's quotation of Isaiah 6:9-10 as a declaration that God has "closed the door" on the Jewish people. What indications, in the larger contexts of both the book of Isaiah and the Acts, suggest that this is not a necessary interpretation of Acts 28?

INDEX OF CITATIONS FROM THE
CATECHISM OF THE CATHOLIC CHURCH

The arabic number(s) following the citation refers to the paragraph number(s) in the *Catechism of the Catholic Church.* The asterisk following a paragraph number indicates that the citation has been paraphrased.

Acts of the Apostles

Citation	Reference
1:1-2	512
1:3	659*
1:6-7	672*
1:7	474,* 673
1:8	672,* 730,* 735, 857,* 1287*
1:9	659,* 697
1:10-11	333*
1:11	665*
1:14	726, 1310,* 2617,* 2623, 2673*
1:22	523,* 535,* 642,* 995
2:1-4	1287*
2:1	2623
2:3-4	696
2:11	1287
2:17-21	715*
2:17-18	1287*
2:21	432,* 2666*
2:22	547
2:23	597,* 599
2:24	633,* 648*
2:26-27	627
2:33	659,* 788*
2:34-36	447,* 449*
2:36-38	1433*
2:36	440, 597,* 695,* 731,* 746
2:38	1226, 1262,* 1287,* 1427*
2:41	363,* 1226*
2:42-46	2178*
2:42	3,* 857,* 949, 1329,* 1342, 2624
2:46	584,* 1329,* 1342
2:47	2640*
3:1	584*
3:9	2640*
3:13-14	597*
3:13	599
3:14	438, 601*
3:15-16	2666*
3:15	612, 626, 632, 635
3:17-18	591,* 600*
3:17	597
3:18	601*
3:19-21	674
4:10	597*
4:11	756*
4:12	432, 452, 1507*
4:20	425
4:21	2640*
4:26-27	436*
4:27-28	600
4:32	952, 2790
4:33	995*
5:12	699*
5:18-20	334*
5:20	584*
5:21	584*
5:28	597*
5:29	450,* 2242, 2256
5:30	597*
5:41	432*
6:6	2632*
6:7	595
7:52	597,* 601*
7:53	332*
7:56	659*
7:60	2635*
8:9-24	2121*
8:12-13	1226*
8:14-17	1315
8:15-17	1288*
8:17-19	699*
8:20	2121
8:26-29	334*
8:32-35	601*
8:37	454*
9:3-18	639*
9:4-5	598*
9:13	823*
9:14	432*
9:20	442
9:34	1507*
10:3-8	334*
10:35	761
10:38	438, 453, 486, 1289
10:39	597*
10:41	659,* 995

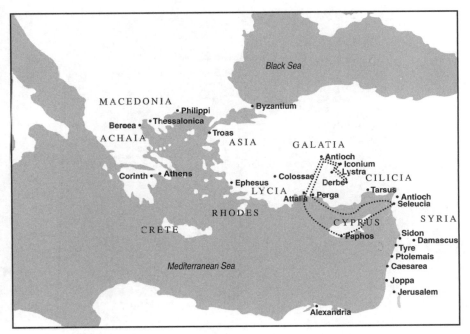

First Journey of Paul

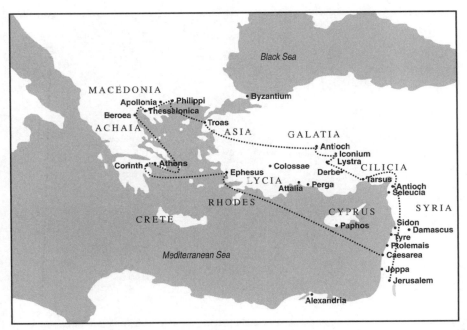

Second Journey of Paul

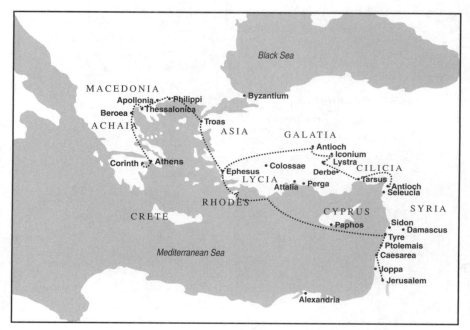

Third Journey of Paul

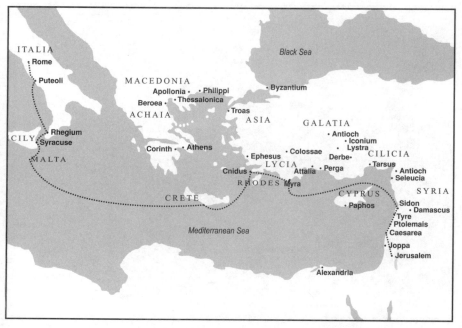

Paul's Journey to Rome

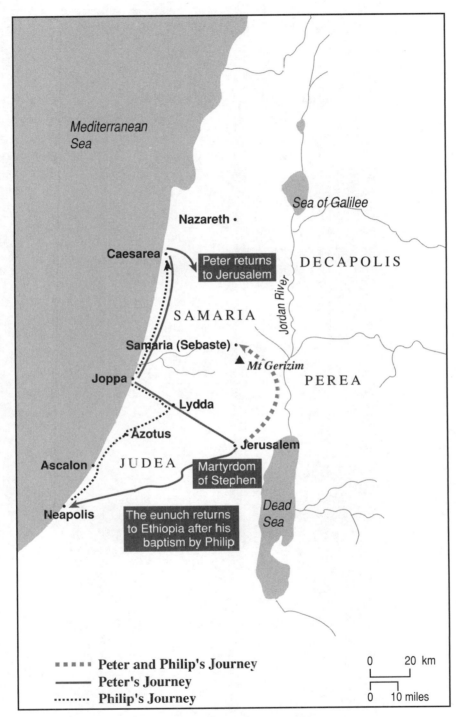

Mediterranean
Sea

Sea of Galilee

Nazareth •

Caesarea •   Peter returns
              to Jerusalem   DECAPOLIS

              SAMARIA

Samaria (Sebaste) •
              ▲ Mt Gerizim   PEREA
Joppa •
        • Lydda

    • Azotus
              Jerusalem •
Ascalon •   JUDEA
              Martyrdom
              of Stephen

Neapolis •   The eunuch returns   Dead
              to Ethiopia after his Sea
              baptism by Philip

▪▪▪▪▪ **Peter and Philip's Journey**   0   20 km
──── **Peter's Journey**
········ **Philip's Journey**   0   10 miles

Journeys of Peter and Philip